PRASE FOR N

"Nothing is more tragic than the separat[...] [...]ave witnessed firsthand the unwavering fai[...] [...] [...] by Kenneth Bae and his family in their quest to bring him home. As a Korean War veteran in Congress, I have been working hard to encourage peace on the Korean Peninsula and to reunite divided families. Inspiring stories like this keep the hope and pulse alive of seeing a unified Korea in our lifetime."

—REP. CHARLES B. RANGEL
MEMBER OF US CONGRESS (1971–2016)

"If you ever have the feeling of being deserted, this is the book you must read. This ordinary man's extraordinary experience with God during the 735 days of his captivity in North Korea shows God's presence, love, and care for us, no matter the situation we are in or who we are. Kenneth Bae's story is evidence of how God brings light and hope even in the darkest tunnel.

"I also desperately sought God's answer during my 140 days in North Korea. *Not Forgotten* carried the answers with the Bible verses that open every chapter. The Lord was and is with me."

—EUNA LEE, JOURNALIST
AUTHOR OF *The World is Bigger Now: An American
Journalist's Release from Captivity in North Korea*

"Kenneth Bae's memoir takes us to the heart of darkness that is North Korea. His account of his two-year detention in North Korea shines a light on this secretive country and its savage treatment of its starving people."

—MELANIE KIRKPATRICK
AUTHOR OF *Escape from North Korea: The Untold
Story of Asia's Underground Railroad*

"As someone who worked to secure Mr. Bae's release, I could only imagine the difficulties, fear, and suffering he endured. *Not Forgotten* gives us an honest glimpse of his experience and of what life is like for ordinary North Koreans, from government officials to prison guards to gas station attendants. His story reveals how his unwavering faith allowed him to act with humility and treat everyone he encountered with compassion. *Not Forgotten* is a story of human hope, perseverance, and triumph."

—GRACE JI-SUN KIM, PH.D.
AUTHOR AND ASSOCIATE PROFESSOR OF THEOLOGY,
EARLHAM SCHOOL OF RELIGION

"In many ways, this is a very personal book for me. While I did not personally know Kenneth prior to being with his family to welcome him home, I had the privilege of being the pastor to Kenneth's family during his imprisonment in North Korea. As such, I intimately knew the ordeal, tears, tenacity, and faith that was involved during his journey. What amazed me then—and today—is that Kenneth and his family continue to pray for the people of North Korea. This is a book not only about the details of a missionary's imprisonment but, more importantly, about God's love for people."

—EUGENE CHO
SENIOR PASTOR, QUEST CHURCH
AUTHOR OF *Overrated: Are We More in Love With the Idea of Changing the World Than Actually Changing the World?*

"An uplifting and Scripture-filled account. Kenneth Bae's witness and testimony to the Lord's presence in his trial is a blessing. It both affirms the faithful goodness of God and allows those of us at home to know that Kenneth never felt abandoned, that prayer can reach beyond the bars of persecution."

—LISA JONES
EXECUTIVE DIRECTOR, CHRISTIAN FREEDOM INTERNATIONAL

"Christians around the world will be blessed by this account of courage for Christ in faithful dependence upon his unwavering grace. Kenneth Bae's love for his North Korean brothers and sisters through years of imprisonment and hard labor powerfully displays the heart of his Savior."

—BRYAN CHAPELL
PASTOR, GRACE PRESBYTERIAN CHURCH
PRESIDENT EMERITUS, COVENANT THEOLOGICAL SEMINARY

NOT FORGOTTEN

NOT FORGOTTEN

THE TRUE STORY OF MY IMPRISONMENT IN NORTH KOREA

KENNETH BAE
WITH MARK TABB

W PUBLISHING GROUP

AN IMPRINT OF THOMAS NELSON

Published in Nashville, Tennessee, by W Publishing, an imprint of Thomas Nelson.

Published in association with Alive Communications, Inc., 7680 Goddard Street, Suite 200, Colorado Springs, CO 80920. www.alivecommunications.com.

Thomas Nelson titles may be purchased in bulk for educational, business, fund-raising, or sales promotional use. For information, please e-mail SpecialMarkets@ ThomasNelson.com.

Scripture quotations are taken from the Holy Bible, New International Version®, NIV®. Copyright © 1973, 1978, 1984, 2011 by Biblica, Inc.® Used by permission of Zondervan. All rights reserved worldwide. www.zondervan.com. The "NIV" and "New International Version" are trademarks registered in the United States Patent and Trademark Office by Biblica, Inc.®

Any Internet addresses, phone numbers, or company or product information printed in this book are offered as a resource and are not intended in any way to be or to imply an endorsement by Thomas Nelson, nor does Thomas Nelson vouch for the existence, content, or services of these sites, phone numbers, companies, or products beyond the life of this book.

ISBN 978-0-7180-7963-5 (HC)
ISBN 978-0-7180-7964-2 (eBook)
ISBN 978-0-7180-8111-9 (IE)

Library of Congress Cataloging-in-Publication Data

Library of Congress Control Number: 2015960286

Printed in the United States of America

16 17 18 19 20 RRD 10 9 8 7 6 5 4

For my sister, Terri, who dedicated her life
for two years to get me home;
for my family, who together hoped and endured suffering;
and for all who stood with me and remembered
me during the darkest time of my life.

"Return home and tell how much God has done for you."
—LUKE 8:39

CONTENTS

Foreword by Bill Richardson xi

Note to the Reader xv

Prologue xvii

Chapter 1: Welcome to Villa Three 1

Chapter 2: The Interrogations Begin 11

Chapter 3: Standing at His Feet 23

Chapter 4: Coming Clean 31

Chapter 5: The Power of Prayer 39

Chapter 6: Operation Jericho 49

Chapter 7: Confession 57

Chapter 8: On to Pyongyang 67

Chapter 9: Far from Home 81

Chapter 10: First Contact 93

Chapter 11: Out for Blood 103

Chapter 12: Guilty as Charged 113

Chapter 13: 103 127

Chapter 14: Down on the Farm 137

Chapter 15: The Whole World Now Knows 149

Chapter 16: Going Home? 161

CONTENTS

Chapter 17: I Am a Missionary 169

Chapter 18: A Visit from Home. 179

Chapter 19: More Disappointment 187

Chapter 20: Missionary in Chains. 197

Chapter 21: Is That What Is Going to Happen to Me?. . . . 207

Chapter 22: Not Alone 219

Chapter 23: I Will Bring You Home 227

Epilogue 237

Acknowledgments 241

Notes 245

About the Authors 247

FOREWORD ────────────────────────────────

FORMER GOVERNOR OF NEW MEXICO BILL RICHARDSON

OVER THE COURSE of my career, I've been called upon to negotiate the release of American prisoners held captive in foreign countries. It is a privilege I never anticipated having and one that I now deeply treasure. At the request of my superiors, even the president, I've flown to some of the most dangerous nations on earth—Cuba, Sudan, Iraq, and North Korea to name a few—to negotiate the release of American citizens. Often, I went after several other envoys made unsuccessful attempts to secure their freedom.

North Korea is at the top of that list. Not only is it very difficult to get into the DPRK, but if you do get in, it can be incredibly difficult to get out. And because the United States has no official relationship with their government, it makes it that much more difficult to communicate and bring about a successful negotiation.

That is why when I learned of Kenneth Bae's arrest, I knew he was in for a difficult journey. I also knew the North Koreans pay close attention to American media, so I quickly spoke out on Kenneth's behalf, along with many other concerned leaders, such as Jesse Jackson and even President Obama. We knew it was going to take some time to figure out a negotiating strategy. Then former NBA star Dennis Rodman launched his own goodwill tour of North Korea, and the publicity for Kenneth's case went to a whole new level. Suddenly we had "sports diplomacy" working for us.

The American people care a great deal about our family members who travel abroad. It has certainly been true of the families of our troops over the decades, and it's been the same with Kenneth's family. The way Kenneth's family and friends organized and brought attention to Kenneth's plight was impressive and did a lot to cause our government to act.

He may be a different kind of soldier, no doubt, but a very effective one nonetheless. You see, I believe in the power and necessity of Americans to get involved in foreign affairs. We need to know other countries, make friends with them, and learn about their leaders, their customs, and their languages. You may not be as bold as Kenneth, but there is a place for ordinary citizens in international relations. We need to grow our list of goodwill ambassadors around the globe to include people driven by humanitarian missions and organizations not sponsored by a government office. Kenneth was and is driven by his strong Christian faith to help the poor and suffering in the far corners of the world. We can learn a lot from his example.

America is blessed with so many citizens with genuine concern for people living under oppressive regimes. They have big hearts and want to help in some way. And that's what I found in Kenneth Bae: a man with a great deal of concern for the poor, starving people suffering under a brutal regime. Not many folks actually want to go to North Korea, but through his deep desire to help and his deep faith, this man found a way to reach them.

Imprisonment is a strange thing. Yes, it is deplorable that a man is held against his will in a foreign land and shoved into forced labor. It can crush the best of us. But there is a way to make the best of a bad situation. Cruel dictators know if they can crush a man's spirit, they will lower his will to live. He can fall into despair in intense isolation. He might go mad thinking he may never see his wife and children again. Or, like Kenneth, he can take his eyes off of his own suffering and begin asking how he might best use his time in this terrible situation. As demonstrated by the experience of the apostle Paul in the Bible, extended amounts of time in prison can have the opposite effect. Instead of endless depression, prisoners can find themselves in long conversations with the prison guards and even form new friendships. Kenneth handled his imprisonment in a model fashion. He remained calm, was cooperative, told the truth, and did what his captors asked him to do. He showed respect to them and did his best to work with them.

We need more people like Kenneth Bae. I believe you will find his story riveting and the lengths he went to help others very inspirational.

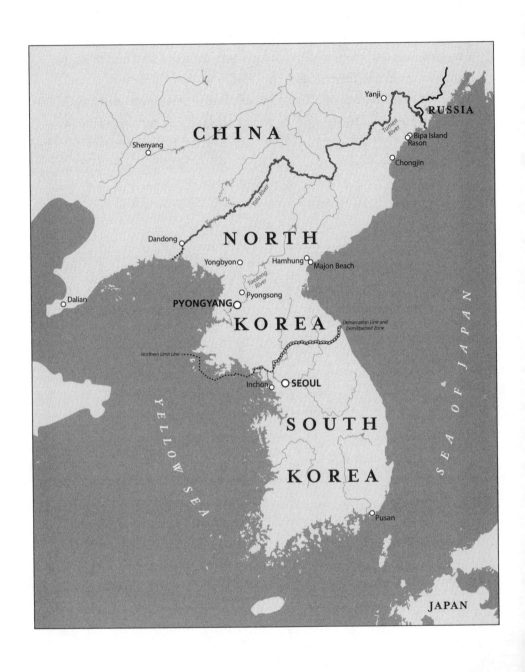

NOTE TO THE READER ————————————

THE NAMES OF and details related to some individuals and locations in this book have been changed to protect their identities. All scriptures used in this book are ones that the author received while meditating on the Bible during his detention in North Korea.

PROLOGUE

A FEW WEEKS before I started writing this book, I began thinking about traveling overseas again. As a missionary, I have a long list of places where I would like to travel and work. However, before I can travel to any other country for an extended period of time, I must obtain a visa. Every visa application includes the question, "Have you ever been convicted of a crime?" The application does not ask if the conviction was justified or if the rest of the world condemned the imprisonment. All it asks is, "Have you ever been convicted of a crime?"

I have to answer truthfully. I must check the *yes* box.

A second question always follows the first: "If yes, what was your crime?"

I don't know how to answer. If I tell the truth, I don't think any country will grant me a visitor visa. According to my prison record, I am a terrorist charged with and convicted of plotting and working to overthrow the government of the Democratic People's Republic of Korea (DPRK), also known as North Korea. After my arrest the prosecutor told me I was the most dangerous American criminal apprehended in the sixty years since the Korean War permanently divided the Korean Peninsula. If I had not been an American citizen, I may have received the death penalty or, at the very least, life in prison with no possibility of parole. Instead, I was sentenced to fifteen years of hard labor.

What did I do that posed such a danger to North Korea? What were my terrorist activities?

I am a missionary.

To the DPRK government, being a missionary is the same as being a terrorist. The terms are interchangeable. As you will discover in the pages that follow, the government finds the gospel of Jesus Christ to be very dangerous. They understand that if they allow the message of Jesus to spread, their government will collapse, along with every aspect of their society. I was tried and convicted of plotting to overthrow the government, even though I never gave away a single Bible or held even one outreach service for the North Korean people. All I did was bring visitors into the country to pray for the North Korean people. That was enough to convict me.

The communist regime in the DPRK has always viewed Christianity as a threat. Ironically, before World War II, when there was only one Korea, more Christians lived in the north than the south. A huge revival broke out in Pyongyang in 1907, with thousands of people coming to Christ. The revival earned Pyongyang the name "Jerusalem of the Far East."

Today, very few people remember that revival ever took place. All those who lived through it are long since dead. But God has not forgotten the work he once did there. My crime was to walk through that land and pray God would do again what he once did. That made me a terrorist and a dangerous criminal.

I guess I still am, because I am still praying for North Korea.

I love the North Korean people, and I hope to return there someday. As you read my story, you will get a glimpse of what life is like for average citizens in one of the most secretive nations on earth. The people have not chosen this life. They live in darkness, completely cut off from the rest of the world. All they know, all they believe, is the propaganda that comes at them all day, every day, through their radios and televisions and schools and newspapers and every other information outlet. They have forgotten life before the days of their Great Leader, life when the light once shone.

As you read the story that follows, I pray that you, too, will fall in love with the North Korean people. They have no voice, but together we can be that voice. God has not forgotten the North Korean people. I write this book so that you will not forget them either.

Welcome to Villa Three

"But when they arrest you, do not worry about what to say or how to say it. At that time you will be given what to say, for it will not be you speaking, but the Spirit of your Father speaking through you."

—MATTHEW 10:19–20

THE MOMENT THE car pulled into the parking lot I knew I was in trouble.

"Are you Mr. Bae?" asked a fiftysomething man who had just stepped out of the black compact sedan that now blocked my path.

From his black suit, white shirt, and black tie, I immediately knew he was a government agent. Like nearly everyone I had met in North Korea, he was very thin. Another, younger man approached me from the other side. He looked to be maybe thirty. Neither one smiled or showed any sign of emotion. They clearly were on a mission.

"I said, are you Mr. Bae?" the first man repeated, even though I could tell he knew the answer.

I swallowed hard. "Yes," I said with a smile, trying to act relaxed, while inside I wanted to panic.

Even before the car pulled into the hotel parking lot, I knew something like this was going to happen. I wasn't sure if it would happen today or tomorrow or the next day, but I was certain that before my scheduled four-day visit was over, government agents would come for me. The only question was when.

"You need to come with us," the man said. His tone of voice told me that if I knew what was good for me, I would do as I was told.

Even so, I hesitated. It felt like a scene from a movie: the black sedan, the agents in dark suits. I'd seen this movie before, and I knew things never turned out too well for the man forced into the backseat of the car.

Before I could say or do anything, the younger man grabbed my arm and pulled me toward the sedan. "Get in now," he growled.

Every outside visitor is accompanied by a government minder, a low-level official whose job is to monitor the visitor's activities and report back to Pyongyang. My minder, who was walking across the parking lot with me, instinctively took a step back as if he didn't know me. I could tell he wished he had never been assigned to my tour group.

"Who are you? Are you part of his tour company?" the younger agent barked at him.

"No," the minder replied. "I am the—"

The first agent cut him off. "Why were the two of you walking around out here?" He didn't have to say it, but I could tell the agent was accusing the minder of breaking some rule. Without waiting for the minder to answer, the agent snapped, "Come with us." Then, as if the minder had any questions about whom the agent was talking to, the agent pointed at him and repeated, "You. Come."

All the color drained from the minder's face. He walked over to the car and climbed in the front seat. His expression told me he was afraid for his life.

The younger agent shoved me into the backseat and climbed in beside me. The older agent got in on the opposite side. Both men's shoulders squeezed up against me as the three of us struggled to fit. The moment the doors closed, the driver sped off.

I watched the passing landscape out the window. Since this was my fifteenth trip to the city of Rason, North Korea, in less than two years,

I knew the place well. Rason is a special economic zone where outside entities can establish businesses. It is the most open city in the country and a place where tourists are allowed, albeit on a limited basis. Through my company, Nations Tours, I had brought three hundred visitors into the country to marvel at its beautiful landscape and to experience its culture while embracing the people of North Korea.

Ten minutes later we passed through the city center without stopping and headed north toward the countryside. I was surprised. I was certain they would take me to some sort of police station for questioning.

No one had yet said a word. The two agents sat perfectly still, all business. The minder in the front seat had not moved either. He had not even glanced over at the driver or looked around to see where we were going. I don't think he wanted to know.

As the car kept going north, I finally broke the silence. "Are we going to the border?" I asked. To me, the question made perfect sense. This whole mess had started eight hours earlier at the border crossing.

"Be quiet and don't say anything," the older agent barked at me.

I sat back in the seat and did as I was told. The car made a right turn and started heading east, toward the coast. I had been this way several times. Just off the coast sits Bipa Island, which is a popular tourist spot. It is the only place in all of Korea where you can see a colony of sea lions.

I don't know why I thought about sea lions at that moment. I knew I was in trouble. I just didn't realize how serious it was.

The road toward the coast went up over a mountain. The driver then turned into the parking lot of the Bipa Hotel, which is tucked into the mountainside near the ocean. A few months earlier I had stayed at this very hotel with one of my tour groups. The hotel, which is about twenty-five miles from the Chinese and Russian borders and six miles from downtown Rason, is made up of three separate villas. Villa One is basically a shrine. The Great Leader, Kim Il Sung, stayed there twice back in the early 1970s. His room is now eternally preserved as a historical landmark. For an extra hundred dollars a night, you can stay in that very room and sleep in the same bed where the Great Leader once slept.

The tour group had not wanted to pay extra to stay in his room. Instead, we stayed in Villa Two, which had been recently renovated by a Chinese investor. Some of the rooms are now as nice as any three-star hotel anywhere in Asia, complete with flat-screen televisions and even personal dry saunas in the bathrooms.

Our car drove past the Great Leader's villa and Villa Two and pulled up to Villa Three, which was surrounded by forest. The car stopped, but I was ordered to stay where I was while the older agent went inside. A few minutes later two men dressed in plain Mao suits with mandarin collars came out and escorted me into the building.

The minder remained in the car. I never saw him again.

"Take off your shoes," one of the men in Mao suits said as we stepped into the entryway of the villa. I did as I was told. The man grabbed my shoes and disappeared with them.

"Come with me," the other man said. He led me down a hallway and into a two-bedroom suite. A luxury hotel this was not. He led me through the spartan living room and the first bedroom and into a second room at the end of a hall. It looked more like a dorm room than a hotel. The three beds, the desk, and the two lounge chairs looked as though they hadn't been replaced since the Great Leader's visit to Villa One. The finished concrete floor did not have a rug or carpet or even tile. A single window looked out on the forest, but most of the window was covered with plastic, preventing me from looking out. A handful of officials were in the suite, with others just outside in the hallway.

"Take off your pants," an official ordered.

I hesitated. The room felt like a walk-in freezer. Temperatures in early November in this part of North Korea drop well below freezing, and it seemed the heat had not yet been turned on. I had on a thin pair of long johns under my trousers, but it was not nearly enough to keep me warm.

"Take off your pants," he repeated.

I did not argue. I slipped off my pants and stood in the middle of the room, shivering. The only possible reason for taking them was to keep me from trying to escape, as if that were even possible. If I could somehow manage to get out of the building unnoticed, I could not go outside and blend in. I was much heavier than the average North Korean man. During my seventeen previous trips inside the country, I learned you could tell how high up in the Labor Party one was by his build. The very few with real influence and power were heavy; everyone else looked to be on the edge of malnutrition. No one was ever going to mistake me for a party official in spite of my weight.

The man who took my shoes returned to the room. He grabbed my pants and left again.

The other man wearing a Mao suit looked me over and said, "Sit in that chair and wait for instructions."

I sat down on a cold, wooden chair across from a desk. A chill crawled up my spine. I'm not sure if it was the cold or fear. I tried to keep from shivering, but sitting on a cold chair in a walk-in freezer without my pants or shoes finally got the best of me.

A few minutes later the older agent who brought me to the villa in the car walked in. He gave some instructions to the other men in the room. I was too nervous to pay much attention to what he said, but everyone else did. They immediately did what he told them to do. Their obedience told me he was the most senior official in the facility.

The senior agent took a seat directly across from me. He stared at me as if I should have known what he was about to say. Finally, he spoke.

"You have carried some very disruptive materials into our great nation, materials filled with lies about our Supreme Leader, Kim Jong Un, and how he cares for us." He paused. "You are going to be our guest here until you explain why you, someone who has been welcomed into our great nation many times, would bring in such materials and what you planned to do with them."

My heart sank. *They've gone through it already*, I thought.

"It" was an external hard drive I had inadvertently carried into North Korea with me. I had it only because I had purchased a new laptop and needed to transfer all my files from the external drive to the new machine.

The trip from my base of operations in Dandong, China, to the border crossing just north of Rason takes twenty-three hours, twenty-one of which are spent on a train from Dandong to Yanji. I planned on transferring everything during the train ride and leaving both my computer and the hard drive in a hotel safe on the Chinese side of the border. Unfortunately, I never got around to transferring the files, and I completely forgot about the hard drive until I opened my briefcase for customs at the border. By then it was too late.

When the customs agents opened the files on the hard drive, they would have found detailed descriptions of six years of mission work in China, along with two years of work in North Korea. All the files were English, which meant they did not yet know what they had. If English files were the only things on the hard drive, I might have been able to stay out of trouble. Unfortunately, I also had more than eight thousand photos and video clips, including photos of other missionaries working in China and in North Korea. The videos included footage from *Inside North Korea*, a 2009 National Geographic Channel documentary that showed starving North Korean children digging in the dirt in search of something to eat.

I knew I could never give an explanation that would satisfy this man, or anyone else in this country, as to why I had the hard drive with me. If I told him the truth—if I said to him, "This is all just a big misunderstanding. I never intended to bring anything disruptive or controversial into North Korea. I threw that hard drive into my briefcase right before I left home and forgot all about it until I found it when I came through customs. There's no sinister plan. Just an honest mistake"—he would not believe me.

"Well," the senior agent said, "can you explain why you brought these materials into our great nation?"

Rather than offer up any excuses, I simply said, "No."

"We will have someone bring your suitcase over from the other hotel," he said in a way that made it sound as though I were now a guest in this villa rather than a prisoner. "Your dinner will be brought in soon," he added and then stood and left.

About fifteen minutes later a guard brought in a bowl of food. He placed it before me and walked out. I stared down at a little glob of rice with a few limp vegetables on top, along with a tiny bit of fried fish that looked more like bait than dinner. Altogether I had maybe six or seven spoonfuls of food.

I didn't feel much like eating, but I tried to force it down. I heard the guards eating their meals in the other room. I assumed they had the same portions as me. When they were still eating twenty minutes later, I realized hunger was one of the tools they planned to use to get information out of me.

All through dinner, and for about half an hour after, I sat in the same wooden chair I had been ordered into when I had first come into the room. The wood was not as cold, but my body ached from sitting in one place for so long.

Suddenly a guard came into the room and ordered me to stand up.

I stood.

In walked a very heavy, middle-aged man who looked like a crime boss from *The Sopranos.* As he walked in, the others in the room stepped back and called him *bujang,* which means "director" in Korean. The look on his face told me he was not happy to be out at this hour. Or maybe that was his normal look. Either way, he was the meanest-looking man I had ever encountered in Korea. And the heaviest.

The bujang took a seat on one of the lounge chairs and motioned for me to sit down. The senior agent came back into the room and stood off to one side. The bujang settled into the chair and pulled out a cigarette. "Do you smoke?" he asked as he held the pack toward me so I could grab one if I liked.

"No, but thank you for offering," I said.

The bujang gave me a dismissive look. He lit his cigarette, drew in deeply, and blew the smoke out in my direction. He acted as if he were about to make me an offer I couldn't refuse.

"We're going to conduct an investigation," he informed me. "You brought in a hard drive filled with files, photos, videos. We want to know who is behind this, who gave this to you to bring into our great nation. And we want to know why you would do this, what your purpose is behind this act."

I nodded to show I understood. I didn't say a word.

"My people are professionals. They are very good at extracting the information we want. Eventually they will learn all your secrets, so the sooner you tell the truth, the better off it will be for you." He paused to let his words sink in. He almost seemed to be enjoying himself.

He took another drag on his cigarette. "Now, we aren't going to use force," he said in a tone that made it clear that they could easily change their minds. "No. That's too childish. And besides," he said with a little smile, "we don't need such barbaric methods to find out what we need to know. You will cooperate. I can assure you of that. The sooner you do, the better for all of us." He let the words hang in the air.

I nodded again.

The bujang motioned toward the door. A younger and much smaller man walked in. At maybe 130 pounds, he was literally half the size of the bujang. A dark suit hung on his five-foot-four frame. His glasses gave him a much less threatening look than that of the man who was clearly his boss. The younger man stepped over to a chair near the bujang and sat down in a very stiff, formal way, like a boy who is afraid of his father.

"This will be your investigator," the bujang said. "You need to cooperate with him." The investigator nodded toward the bujang to acknowledge what he had just said.

"Do we start now?" I asked.

"No," the bujang said, "it is too late to get started tonight. We will let you get your rest. Our investigation will begin first thing in the morning." He stood. The investigator immediately jumped to his feet. The guard motioned for me to stand as well, which I did.

"Until then," the bujang continued, "this will be your room. Take the bed there next to the window. Your guards will take the other two beds. The investigation team will be in the next room." With that, the bujang left the room. The investigator and the senior agent followed close behind.

A guard stepped over to me. "Time for bed. You go over there." He pointed toward the third bed.

I walked over and noticed there was only one thin blanket on the bed. I still didn't have my pants. I had on a light jacket that I was wearing when I was picked up in the hotel parking lot, but it wasn't going to help much in this freezing room.

I lay down on the bed and tried to get comfortable under the blanket. I shivered uncontrollably.

"Are you still cold?" one of the guards asked.

"Yes," I replied.

"Okay," the guard said. He left the room and returned with another blanket, but it was no thicker than the one I already had. I wrapped it around myself. My body stopped shaking.

Across the room a guard lay on one of the other two beds. The guard who brought me the blanket sat down and kept watch over me. One of the two was always awake, as if I were dangerous.

Even with the extra blanket I could not sleep. I was worried about my Chinese assistant, Stream, and the four people we had brought in on this tour: two Americans and an Australian man with his German wife. Had they been detained as well? Right after I had discovered the hard drive in my briefcase, I told them to act as though they did not know me and, if asked, to say they had only just met me when the tour began. *Were they able to stick to their story? Are they safe now? Or are they in another room like this somewhere, suffering because of my stupid mistake? Will they be able to leave the country?*

I tossed and turned on my bed, worrying. I had no idea what was going to happen to them or what might have already happened to them.

I thought about my children. My twenty-two-year-old son, Jonathan, and my sixteen-year-old daughter, Natalie, lived in Arizona, while my twenty-year-old stepdaughter, Sophia, lived in Dandong with my wife, Lydia. They had no idea what had happened to me. *I could disappear, and they will think I have just abandoned them. There is so much I want to tell them. Will I ever get the chance?*

Lydia had begged me not to take this trip. "Don't go," she had said. "I need you here." But I had come anyway.

Tears filled my eyes. *Will I ever see my family again?*

My wondering turned into prayer. I had become a Christian shortly before my family moved from Seoul, South Korea, to the United States in 1985. Throughout my life, I had felt God's call, first to China and then to North Korea. Ultimately my faith was what had landed me in this room. Now it would have to sustain me until I could leave.

Help me, Lord, I prayed. *Help me. You always have. You have protected me from harm these past six years during my mission work in China. You have led me down this path, every step of the way. You have never failed to watch over me. Where are you, Lord? I need your help.*

I fell asleep praying.

TWO ————————————————————————

THE INTERROGATIONS BEGIN

Then I heard the voice of the Lord saying, "Whom shall I send?
And who will go for us?"
    And I said, "Here am I. Send me!"

—ISAIAH 6:8

"GET UP AND get ready," a guard said.

I opened my eyes to see a young man in uniform standing over me. For a split second I forgot where I was.

"You have ten minutes to take a shower. Hurry up," he said.

Now I remembered. The bad dream was real.

I stumbled into the bathroom, grateful for the chance to bathe. "Ten minutes," the guard repeated.

However, the shower did not work. Instead, I filled the bathtub with warm water, stood in the middle of the tub, and dumped the water over my head with a bucket. It may not have been a traditional shower, but it left me refreshed.

Standing in the tub, I started praying. *God, give me strength. I do not know what this day holds, but you do. Give me your strength. Put your words in my mouth so that I will know how to answer my accusers.*

Breakfast arrived not long after I finished my shower. It looked exactly like my dinner from the night before, both in size and contents.

It didn't take me long to down it. I still did not have much of an appetite. I was too nervous to think about food.

After breakfast the guard told me to sit and wait. I sat in the same hard chair as I had the night before. It was still cold.

With nothing else to do, my mind raced back to the previous day. I kicked myself for being so careless and not going through my bags before entering the country. I had had plenty of opportunities. I had never opened my briefcase during the train ride from Dandong to Yanji. Nor did I look in it while at the hotel that night, or at any point during the two-hour bus ride from the hotel to the border.

I should have at least gone through my briefcase to make sure all of my group's paperwork was in order. Instead, I had sat toward the front of the bus and chatted away with a friend and fellow missionary, someone I will call Lisa. Lisa was not part of our group. She has her own humanitarian work in North Korea.

Lisa had even given me a chance to check my bags right before we crossed over from China. The bus had stopped at a small convenience store that also had storage lockers. "I'm going to leave my cell phone here," Lisa had said when she got off the bus. "Do you have anything you need to leave behind before we cross the border?"

Without looking through my bags, I had said, "No, I'm good."

How could I have been so careless? I screamed at myself. If this had been my first trip into North Korea instead of my eighteenth, I probably would have done a quick double check. But by that point I had become so comfortable that I never thought something from home that I didn't want to take in might have been in my bags.

I replayed the scene over and over as I waited (for what, I did not know). I imagined DPRK government agents going through each and every file and all the photos on my hard drive, studying every face and making a list of everyone they were going to go after as coconspirators.

And what will happen when they translate the files? Everything about my work in both China and North Korea was in those files. I knew it was just a matter of time until they discovered the full truth about who I was and what I had been doing in Korea. *Then what?* I wondered. *What will they do to me?*

I knew what they had done to others. Growing up in South Korea, I had heard the stories of how people just disappear up here.

But I wasn't nervous for just myself. I was nervous for everyone who had been in contact with me since I had brought my first tour group into North Korea two years earlier. Specifically, I thought of Sam, who owned the coffee shop in the hotel in Rason where I had been arrested. Born in China, he had become a Christian and had served on staff in my mission center in Dandong. He now split his time between Dandong and Rason. I hated to think what might happen to him if his cover were blown. The moment the authorities translated my files, they would investigate him because of his relationship with me.

Then there was another North Korean, Songyi. I had met her while she was in China on a visitor visa. After returning to her North Korean home, she had tried to start a Christian orphanage. Because of my hard drive, she was no longer safe. Unlike me, she did not have the protection that comes with being a United States citizen. My files put her at risk, and she would not be hard for the government to find.

My waiting ended when a doctor walked into my room. "I'm going to do a checkup," the doctor said.

I wondered why I was being examined, but I let the doctor do the checkup. "Do you have any known medical conditions?" the doctor asked.

"I have diabetes," I replied, "hyperlipidemia, gallstones, an enlarged prostate, and a fatty liver. I also fell fifteen years ago and hurt my back. It still causes a lot of pain for me."

"Uh-huh," the doctor said as he wrote everything down. "Are you on any medications?"

"I am for my diabetes, gallstones, and high cholesterol," I replied.

"Do you have those with you?"

"They're in my suitcase."

The doctor took more notes. "Okay," he said. "I think you will be fine here."

I did not find his words reassuring.

After the doctor left, another official came and dropped off an itemized list of everything in my suitcase. Then the investigator I had met the night before came back into my room. I was seated in the same wooden chair next to the desk. I overheard another official call him by name, which is how I learned his name was Mr. Park. (He never introduced himself to me. Later, when I asked if this was his name, he denied it.)

Mr. Park seemed to be in a good mood as he sat down across from me. He placed a new spiral notebook in front of him in which to take notes. I recognized it. It had been in my suitcase the day before.

"Did you sleep well last night?" he asked.

"Yes," I lied. I didn't want to tell him I had tossed and turned with worry all night. That would only make me look guilty.

"Good, good," he said. "We want you to be comfortable while you are our guest. Now I have some questions for you. If you cooperate, this shouldn't take long."

I nodded. At this stage I did not plan to admit to anything more than being a businessman who had contributed to the local economy through my company, Nations Tours. Yes, I would admit, I had made an honest mistake carrying into the country an external hard drive that contained materials that appear to be subversive, but I never intended to share this material with anyone.

"Now, rather than sit and talk, I find it is more helpful if you write out your answers. Take as much time as you need to really think about what you want to say," Mr. Park said as he placed a small stack of computer paper, along with a pen, in front of me. I recognized the pen as well. It was one of mine.

"We will begin by you telling us a little more about yourself." His tone and demeanor struck me as the complete opposite of the bujang, who had come across like a crime boss. "Please tell me about your family. Tell me a little about your relatives, where they live, what they do in their jobs, and their experiences. When you are finished writing, raise your hand, and I will come get your paper."

That last line surprised me. I felt as though I had been kicked back down to grade school.

I picked up the pen and thought about what to include. Mr. Park stood and walked toward the door. "Take as much time as you need," he said with a smile.

Although I am an American citizen, my family's roots go back to Yongbyon, a small city about sixty miles north of Pyongyang, in what is now North Korea. There was only one Korea, then known as Chosun, when my family migrated there from the southern end of the Korean Peninsula more than 150 years ago. For four generations before my paternal grandfather, my family lived and worked in Yongbyon.

The country changed a great deal during that time. The first missionaries came to Korea in 1885. Today, many people in the West know about the large number of Christians and churches in South Korea. What most do not realize is that the northern part of Korea was where the gospel first took root. In 1907 a revival broke out in Pyongyang, and tens of thousands of people came to Christ.

Even as Christianity spread, times remained difficult in all of Korea. In 1904 the Japanese Empire forced the Korean king to sign an agreement that essentially stripped Korea of her independence. By 1910 Japan had annexed all of Korea. The country suffered greatly under Japanese rule. Unfortunately for my family, when Japan surrendered to the United States at the end of World War II, life did not get much better. In 1945, the United States and the Soviet Union divided the Korean Peninsula in two at the thirty-eighth parallel, which put my family's home in Yongbyon right in the middle of the communist North.

The division into two Koreas was supposed to be temporary, lasting only until the United Nations could organize and hold free elections for all of Korea to set up a unified government. But the Soviet Union blocked the plan, and by 1948 they had installed a Marxist government in the north under the control of Kim Il Sung. He proclaimed himself the Great Leader and, over time, put in place what is basically a religious system where he was, and still is, a god for North Koreans.

The communist ideology later developed into what is called *juche*, which is pronounced "ju-chay." The word means "self-reliance," but the concept is built upon the idea that the Great Leader is all anyone really needs. When the Soviets pulled out of the country in 1949, they left Kim Il Sung with all he needed in terms of heavy artillery, tanks, airplanes for an air force, and extensive training for his troops.

My family's fortunes turned when Kim Il Sung's DPRK army invaded South Korea on June 25, 1950. Three days later communist troops had overrun South Korea's capital, Seoul. American president Harry Truman immediately sent troops over from Japan, but they didn't make much difference at first. By the end of July 1950, Kim Il Sung controlled all of Korea except a very small area around the port city of Pusan on the southern tip of the Korean Peninsula. Then Douglas MacArthur arrived.

On September 15 the United States Marines landed in Inchon, just south of Seoul and well behind enemy lines. Under MacArthur's command, American and United Nations forces drove Kim Il Sung's armies back across the thirty-eighth parallel in a matter of weeks. By the end of November, American troops had taken nearly all of Korea, all the way to the Chinese border on the Yalu River and well north of my family. Then China entered the war and the front line started moving back south.

When my paternal grandparents realized the war was moving back toward them, my grandfather loaded his family and everything they could carry into his truck and moved south to Pyongyang, which United Nations troops controlled at the time. My great-grandmother stayed home in Yongbyon to watch over the house. My great-grandfather and the rest of the family thought that if they stayed in Pyongyang for a week or two, the battle lines would push back north again and they could go home. When the UN forces retreated to the south, our family had to go with them in order to avoid the conflict, leaving behind my great-grandmother.

No one in our family ever saw her again.

Eventually my family ended up in Pusan. They later moved to Seoul after the war.

My father was only six years old when he fled North Korea with his family. He grew up in Seoul and met my mother there. My dad was a famous baseball player and later a professional manager, one of the best in all the country. I was born in 1968 and spent my first sixteen years in Seoul as well.

I did not include all of this information in the papers I wrote for Mr. Park. If he discovered my family had purposely fled from North Korea to South Korea during the war, his attitude toward me might well take a turn for the worse. I saw no sense in aggravating him if I didn't need to. Instead, I wrote that my family's life had been disrupted by the war and we ended up in Seoul. I also wrote of my immediate family moving to the United States in 1985, when I was sixteen, so that my sister and I could receive a better education.

We first moved to San Jose, California, where one of my uncles lived. None of us spoke much English at all, even though I took English as a Second Language classes for a few months right before we left Korea. Once we arrived in San Jose, I found I was one of very few Korean students in my high school. The teachers struggled to correctly pronounce my given name, Junho. Calling roll they always called me Juno, which is a girl's name. (Years later, when I became a naturalized US citizen, I decided it was time to have an American name. I picked Kenneth because I had never heard anyone mispronounce Kenneth. Also, I didn't know any other Kenneths at the time.)

After about a year we moved from San Jose to Torrance, in the Los Angeles area, which had a much larger Korean population. My English improved, and I graduated from West Torrance High School in 1988.

The summer before my family and I moved to the United States, I was a new Christian. Our youth group in Seoul had a dynamic leader who challenged us to seek God's direction for our lives. When I heeded his challenge, I heard God say to me, *Shepherd*. No other words came.

Just *shepherd*. Since shepherd and pastor are synonymous, I knew God was calling me to some kind of pastoral work.

That calling became a little clearer the summer after graduation, when I attended a retreat organized by Campus Crusade for Christ (also known as CCC or Cru), one of the largest college ministries in the world. Dr. Bill Bright, the founder, spoke and challenged a large group of us to embrace China. I felt God call me there.

Yes, Lord, I will go to China for you, I prayed.

That summer, I traveled to Seoul to visit family. I went to bookstores and bought every book I could find on China. When I went off to college at the University of Oregon, I planned on studying psychology but minoring in Chinese to further prepare me for what I believed was going to be my life's work.

Two weeks after school started, I met a girl, and we started dating. A year later we got married. I pretty much forgot about China.

We had our first child, Jonathan, in 1990, not long after we got married. For a time I dropped out of school to support the family, but I eventually graduated from San Francisco Bible College in 1996, the same year our daughter, Natalie, was born. I received a master of divinity degree from Covenant Theological Seminary in St. Louis in 2002.

My marriage fell apart three years later. I ended up spending a lot of time in Kona, Hawaii, where I felt God renew my call to China. I moved to Dalian, China, in 2006, and then to Dandong, right across the Yalu River from the northwest corner of North Korea.

"I went to China to open a cultural exchange company," I wrote, "then I moved my business to Dandong and expanded it to include a hotel and a touring company, Nations Tours." I went on to write how I met my wife, Lydia, in 2007 in Dandong, where she owned a dress shop. We were married in 2009. "I have a stepdaughter, Sophia," I added.

When I finished, I held up my hand. The parts of my story I felt I needed to include filled about five or six pages of paper. But there was much I had left out. I did not explain that the time I had spent in Hawaii was at a Discipleship Training School (DTS) put on by Youth With A

Mission (YWAM). Nor did I tell them that I was on staff with them. I also did not include the detail that my real reason for moving to China was to start a DTS. I didn't think the details were any of the North Koreans' business.

Mr. Park came back into the room without anyone having to go get him. That told me they had cameras on me, watching my every move.

"Very good, Bae Junho," Mr. Park said, calling me by my Korean name. (In Korean, the family name comes first.) "Now let's see what you have written," he said. He glanced over it quickly before placing more sheets of plain white paper in front of me.

"Now tell me why you brought the hard drive into our great nation," he said in a rather relaxed tone.

I nodded. He walked out with my first essay in his hand. I sat for a moment and thought about how I should phrase this next story. *Just tell the truth*, I felt God whisper to me.

"I never intended to bring disruptive materials across the border," I wrote. "Before bringing any group into the country, I always instructed them on what they could not bring or leave behind. 'Never bring in a computer,' I stressed. 'Never bring in anything that may insult our gracious hosts,' I always said. I violated my most basic rule on this, my eighteenth trip inside the country, purely by accident.

"Shortly before coming on this trip I bought a new laptop computer. I had not had a chance to transfer all my files from my old computer to my new one, which is why I purchased the hard drive. Since my trips into North Korea always begin with a twenty-one-hour train ride from Dandong to Yanji, China, I planned to switch all my files then. I planned on using the hard drive as a backup after my new laptop was up and running.

"Unfortunately, I never got around to moving the files. Instead, I spent my time getting to know the members of my tour group. When I wasn't talking to them, I spent my time learning to use the movie editing software on my new computer. I thought I could take care of it once I arrived at the hotel in Yanji, but we went out to dinner first for a delicious barbecued duck meal as soon as we got into the city. When I got to my hotel room I called my wife on the phone. We talked until I couldn't hold my eyes open. I ended up passing out on my bed with all the lights in my room still on.

"I did not stir until my assistant, Stream, banged on my door at five thirty the next morning, asking if I was going to come downstairs in time to catch the bus that would take us to the border, a two-hour trip. All thoughts of the hard drive left me as I jumped up from the bed, washed my face, and dashed out the door. I handed Stream my laptop before we left and asked her to have the hotel lock it up in their safe until I returned in four days. You may check it if you like," I wrote. "You will find it has very few files on it.

"Once I was up and around I took my group to the bus station. I never even opened my briefcase until we were already in North Korea. I did not remember I had the hard drive until I saw it in my briefcase in customs." This was the honest truth.

I held up my hand to signal I was finished writing. Mr. Park came in and took my paper from me. "Good, good. I look forward to reading your answers," he said. He disappeared into the other room.

I hoped this might be the end of this matter. I knew they had probably already interrogated the North Korean tour guide with whom I had worked on all my trips. He would back up everything I had said. I was a businessman with a good reputation in this city who had made an honest mistake. There was nothing more anyone needed to concern themselves with.

A guard served me lunch, but I did not feel like eating. Shortly after lunch Mr. Park stormed into the room, red faced and angry. This was not the pleasant man who had sat across the desk from me earlier that morning.

"This is no good!" he yelled. "I told you I wanted the truth, not lies! Get up, *now*! Go over there." He pointed to the corner of the room. "Go stand over there until you are prepared to tell us the truth!"

I got up and did as I was told.

"Hands down to your side. Do not move!" he ordered. "You are being punished. You can come out of the corner when you are ready to tell us the real story."

I thought about the movies where police use the good cop, bad cop technique to try to get the information they want. Mr. Park had become both the good cop and the bad cop.

While I stood in the corner, another movie played out in my head, one I hoped was about to come true. I imagined that the computer chip in my passport had been activated the moment I was taken captive. The signal would be picked up by the Marines on the other side of the thirty-eighth parallel. They would relay the signal to the White House, where President Obama would pick up the hotline phone. "Do it," he would tell a general on the other end.

Then a team of Navy Seals would crash through the window of my room in Villa Three, guns drawn. One would rush over to me.

"Are you all right, Mr. Bae?" he would ask.

"I am now," I would reply.

"With the order of the president of the United States, we are here to get you home, sir." The Marines would then lead me to the shore, and we would get on the boat and paddle out to a nearby submarine.

I am going home. Thank you, President Obama, for rescuing me.

Standing in the corner facing the wall, with this movie playing in my head, I smiled. Mr. Park came over to me. "Why are you smiling? Stop it. You are being punished!"

His words snapped me back to reality, but I couldn't help but wonder if my dream was going to come true. I hoped it would, and soon.

STANDING AT HIS FEET

"Do not be afraid of them, for I am with you and will rescue you," declares the LORD.

—JEREMIAH 1:8

I KNEW BEYOND a shadow of a doubt God had called me to North Korea. Seven years ago, while I was living in Kona, Hawaii, I went to Dalian, China, with a YWAM group as a way of dipping my toe into the water of mission work. In my spirit I sensed God renewing the call I felt the summer after high school, a call I had lost sight of when life got in the way.

In November 2005 I traveled from Dalian to Dandong to meet a missionary whom I knew through a mutual friend. I wanted to see the work he was doing. While I was there, I met a North Korean woman who had crossed over to Dandong on a visitor visa a month before. During her first week in China, she met my missionary friend, who told her about Jesus. She immediately gave her life to Christ. When I met her she'd been a Christian for all of three weeks.

After I heard her story, I was so moved that I asked her how I could pray for her. "No, no, no," she said, "don't pray for me. I already have Jesus. Pray for the people of North Korea. They need to know the real God."

Her words blew me away. She had come to China to try to make a little money because her family had nothing, but now that she had Jesus, she was telling me he was all she really needed.

My missionary friend then introduced me to another North Korean, who was also in China on a visitor visa. This man, who was in his mid-fifties, had two children and a wife on the other side of the Yalu River. He, too, came over to China in search of work, but he had not been able to find a job due to health problems. Like the first woman, he first heard about Jesus from my missionary friend, and he didn't waste any time giving his life to Christ.

I asked the man how he now felt about being a Christian. "I did not have hope before, but now I have a hope to live for and a hope to look forward to," he told me.

I sat in awe of this man. His wife and children had no food. He suffered from all sorts of physical problems. But now that he had Jesus, he had hope, something he'd never had before.

These stories were still spinning around in my head when my missionary friend asked if I wanted to go see North Korea up close. Of course I said yes. "You can get within ten feet of the border," he explained. "You can also take a boat that goes across the Yalu River and touches the North Korean shore. If you don't get out of the boat, you are still officially in China, and you should be safe."

He didn't have to say anything more. I needed to go. I needed to see the country where my family had lived.

The next day, after the sun had gone down, I joined a handful of people and stood in the very front of a boat as we crossed a narrow creek, only about fifteen yards wide, that feeds into the Yalu. The Chinese pilot motored along the shore for about ten minutes before pushing the bow of the boat up on the land in North Korea. The pilot then called in Chinese, "Come on out."

Out of the darkness came a very young, very thin, and very tall (at least for Korea) DPRK soldier. As he came into the light of the boat, I could see a machine gun pointed right at us.

"Hi," I said in Korean, trying to remain calm—or at least as calm as you can be when you are staring down the barrel of a gun.

"Do you have any money?" the soldier asked.

Common sense says that if a man with a machine gun pointed at you asks for money, you give him some money. But I said, "No. I'm sorry. We didn't bring any money for you."

"Do you have any cigarettes?"

"No. We don't have any cigarettes," I said. "But we brought this for you." I handed him a sack. "There's some bread and some food, including an apple and beef jerky from the US. There are also some soft drinks." Little bribes like this are what makes it possible for the boat to land on the shore of North Korea.

He grabbed the sack and said, "Thank you." After taking a quick peek inside, he disappeared back into the darkness.

As I watched the soldier go, the Lord spoke to me. *What he needs is not money. It is not cigarettes. He needs Jesus, the only way, the truth, and the life. No one turns to the kingdom of God except through him.*

I answered God right then and there. *Lord, if you want to use me as the bridge connecting North Korea to the outside world, use me. Lord, here I am.*

I did not know it at the time, but the soldier could have arrested me right then and dragged me and everyone else on the boat off to prison. When my friends back in Dalian learned what I had done, they were very angry with me. "Why did you do that? You risked your life for what?!" they said. But I knew God had spoken to me on that boat.

Here I am. Use me as a bridge for North Korea to the world, I prayed.

Five years passed before I entered North Korea again—legally this time. I started a tour company, Nations Tours, and since March 2011 the company had taken three hundred people into North Korea over the course of twenty-three trips. I wanted everyone we took into the country to have the same experience I had on my first visit.

God had not forgotten North Korea. The new Christians I had met in Dandong in 2005 showed me how hungry North Koreans were for the truth. I wanted those I brought to North Korea to see the people and see their need for Jesus.

Now I was deeper into North Korea than I ever imagined possible, surrounded by government agents and high-ranking officials. Some of the most important men in the entire city had been here in my room. And all I got to do was stand in the corner like a naughty little boy.

During my first full day in captivity, I stood in this corner for hours. I stared at the blank wall until the light from outside my window faded into black. I knew the sun went down around six o'clock. Once it was dark outside, one of the guards brought me dinner. I sat down at the desk and ate my six or seven spoonfuls of rice and wilted vegetables and something I thought was a little piece of meat or pork fat. Then it was back to the corner.

I heard the television come on in the other room. In Rason, North Korea's one and only central television station broadcasts only in the evenings during the week. Hours later I heard the DPRK national anthem playing from the television, which meant the broadcasts were done for the day. From my previous trips into the country, I knew it was now ten thirty. I kept standing.

Finally I was allowed to go to bed. I had no idea what time it was, but I knew it was late. I had probably stood in the corner for at least six hours. One guard slept on one of the beds across from me, while the other stood watch. A guard cannot keep watch in the dark, so that meant a light stayed on at all hours.

I had trouble going to sleep. It felt as though I had just drifted off when a guard woke me: "Get up. The investigator will be here soon. You must get ready."

I dragged myself out of bed and took another bucket shower.

This was my second full day of detainment, my second full day of interrogation. Mr. Park had seemed none too pleased with my answers the day before. I dreaded what he might do today. But, rather than panic, a peace came over me. I recalled Matthew 10:19–20, which says, "But when they arrest you, do not worry about what to say or how to say it. At that time you will be given what to say, for it will not be you speaking, but the Spirit of your Father speaking through you."

A guard brought in a meager breakfast, and it didn't take me long to eat it. I was nearly as hungry after breakfast as I was before. But then I remembered Jesus' words when he was tempted in the wilderness: "Man shall not live on bread alone, but on every word that comes from the mouth of God" (Matthew 4:4). Never had these words seemed so true. From that point on, during my entire month in Rason I was seldom hungry or tired. I had a food they didn't know about—Jesus!

At around eight thirty—I guessed based on how long the sun had been up—Mr. Park arrived.

"Okay," he said, "I did not expect you to tell the truth, so I guess I should not be surprised at the lies you wrote yesterday. Today I give you another chance." He slid more paper over to me along with a new pen. "I need you to tell me your background. Give me the names of all your uncles and aunts and cousins in Korea. Where are they, and what are they doing now? And I need the names of your grandparents who you said left our great nation during the Korean War."

"I will do my best," I said.

Mr. Park left, and I started writing. I knew God was going to give me the words I needed, but, for the life of me, I could not remember things I should have known. I forgot the names of my aunts and uncles who still lived in South Korea. Maybe it was the lack of sleep or the lack of food or the stress. Or maybe God just kept me from remembering. Whatever the reason, I knew even before I finished how Mr. Park was going to respond to my latest essay.

I held up my hand, and Mr. Park returned to collect what I had written.

"Stay in that chair," he said. "Do not get up. You have more to write." He gave me still more paper. "You grew up in Namchosun," he said, using the North Korean name for South Korea. "What were you taught in your schools about our great nation? I have talked to many people about you. All say you are a very respectable businessman. That is why we have treated you so well. But something must have made you do this terrible act."

Once more, he left me alone to complete his latest assignment.

I wrote: "I was taught North Korea attacked the south in 1950 and that it remains hostile toward South Korea today. When I lived in Seoul I learned the DPRK continues to carry out terrorist acts against us, including blowing up a commercial airplane and sinking ships. Everyone in South Korea is convinced North Korea still wants to conquer the entire peninsula."

I then wrote about the event that had forever broken my heart for the North Korean people: a severe famine that had hit the DPRK from 1997 to 2002. According to the reports I saw in both the United States and South Korea, more than three million people had starved to death. I did not go into detail, but hearing about the famine had made me very, very upset. I did not understand how any government could do this to its own people. It confirmed every negative thing I had ever heard about the DPRK. Its government not only allowed its people to starve, but it also executed anyone who tried to escape the country. I have seen photographs of dead bodies, of both adults and children, floating in the Yalu River—people who were shot while trying to cross to China.

When Mr. Park read my latest essay, he grew very angry. "These are all lies! We did not attack anyone. We are a peaceful nation. All we've ever wanted is to be left alone. But the United States and Namchosun attacked us. President Kim Il Sung delivered us from the Americans. As for the famine, that is more lies. Yes, people died, but we are not to blame. All fault lies with the Americans."

He fumed with anger and stared at me with a disgusted look on his face.

"Get up. You are to stand there without moving!" he yelled, pointing to a spot in the middle of the room. "Your lies today are worse than your lies yesterday! Stand there and do not move until you are ready to tell us the truth! You are a liar! How dare you insult our nation with such a lie."

I told him that I did not come up with these stories; I was taught them in school and through Western media.

He did not want to listen. "Get up and stand still!"

I stood where he told me to stand. Apparently, simply standing in the corner was not punishment enough. They thought forcing me to stand in one spot without moving a muscle would wear me down physically. It did not. No matter how long I stood in one place, my feet never hurt and my back did not ache. I could have stood there forever, if I had to.

Two revelations came to me. The first was that I was going to lose a lot of weight before this was all over. My family had been after me to get in shape for a long time. I thought, *I am glad I did not listen. Thank God for that extra fifty pounds I've been carrying around. I think it will get me through the winter.*

My second revelation was that I would leave North Korea with a great story to tell. I remembered Luke 8:39, which says, "Return home and tell how much God has done for you." *I'm going to get to do just that!* I thought.

Over the previous six years I had watched God do one amazing thing after another. I wanted to write down those stories to tell the world about God's faithfulness. But now, standing perfectly still, feeling no fatigue, I knew God was giving me an even greater story to tell. I thought of his words to Joshua right before he led the Israelite army into Jericho: "Stand up! What are you doing down on your face?" (Joshua 7:10). That's what I was now doing—standing up for the Lord. But I wasn't just standing up for him; I was standing at his feet.

I knew security cameras were hidden somewhere on the wall. Hour after hour I scanned every inch of it, but I still could not find the cameras.

The room remained uncomfortably cold. It was warmer than it was when I had arrived a couple of days earlier, but it still wasn't over fifty degrees. As I had the first night, I shivered from the cold. But suddenly, my left hand started getting warm. Standing absolutely still, I slowly opened my hand. I saw something sparkling like gold dust. Then, the warmth spread from my hand and up my left arm. I did not know what was happening.

I heard the Lord speak in an unmistakable way. *The Holy Spirit is holding your hand,* his Spirit said to my spirit. *You are not alone. The Holy Spirit is standing next to you, holding your hand. Do not worry about anything.*

No one will harm you through this. Do not worry about what you are to say. I will speak through you, because I am with you and I will never leave you. No one will be harmed. Don't worry about anyone. Just tell the truth.

The warmth in my hand started to fade away, but the sense of God's presence did not. *If the Lord is with me, whom shall I be afraid of?* I thought. *My God has not forsaken nor forgotten me!*

Joy came over me, and I began praising God in my heart. My eyes could not see the Lord, but I felt his arms wrapped around me. God felt so close.

I stood there, enjoying the feel of his arms around me, smiling. I was rejoicing, standing still at his feet.

He is standing next to me. All I have to do is stand at his feet every time I have no control of what is going on. I smiled even more, knowing that God was still in control despite what was happening.

Soon, I heard people talking in the other room. "This isn't working! He is smiling!" someone said.

Mr. Park returned and said, "That's enough. You can go to bed now."

I never had to stand still in the middle of the room or the corner again.

I lay down and silently thanked the Lord: *You know my name. You know my every thought. You are good and gracious. I will not be afraid. I will trust you, Lord. I will stand still at your feet.*

COMING CLEAN

Cast all your anxiety on him because he cares for you.
—1 PETER 5:7

WHEN I WOKE up the next morning, I still had a very strong sense of the Lord's presence. He kept repeating Romans 12:14 to me: *Bless those who persecute you; bless and do not curse.* I had known this verse all my adult life, but it sounded different in light of where I was and what I faced.

Okay, Lord, I prayed, *I will try. But I cannot bless in my own strength. You will have to give me the power, because my flesh wants to curse.*

I thought of 2 Corinthians 12:9, which says, "My grace is sufficient for you, for my power is made perfect in weakness."

I needed as much of God's grace as I could get when Mr. Park came storming into my room. "You are still writing lies," he said waving the pages I had written the day before.

I expected him to usher me to the corner. Instead, he motioned for a guard to come over beside me. Visions of the television show *24*, in which agents use truth serum to get the information they want, flashed in my mind. *I think I watch too much television*, I told myself. I took a deep breath and tried to relax.

"Down on your knees," the guard said.

I got down on the floor, knees against the concrete, and sat back on my heels. "No, not like that. Up," he ordered. I straightened up, standing on my knees as best I could on the cold, hard floor. I wobbled just a bit as I shifted my weight, trying to find a comfortable way to hold this position.

Within a few minutes the muscles in my back started tightening into a knot. The knot kept getting tighter and tighter until the pain became unbearable. I broke out in a sweat, even though the temperature in the room was maybe fifty degrees. My body started to sway. I felt like I might fall over.

I looked up at the guard. "I cannot do this," I said. "I have a back problem. I'm doing the best I can, but I just can't do this."

"Okay then. Get up," the guard said in a disgusted tone. I stood and tried to stretch out the pain in my back. My knees ached as well.

The guard let me stand for maybe ten minutes. Then he barked, "Get down again." I went up and down like that for a couple of hours.

When Mr. Park returned, we went through the writing dance again. This day's questions were basically the same ones he had asked over and over since he started his investigation. I wrote until my hand cramped. I didn't know how many times I could say the same thing.

Just as he had every other time, Mr. Park became red faced and angry when he read my latest essay. "More lies!" he yelled. "You say you brought in the disruptive materials by accident. I do not believe you. How stupid do you think I am? Do you take me to be a fool?"

"You can call my assistant and have her call the hotel in Yanji to release my computer to you," I replied.

I had two reasons for suggesting this. First, I wanted to make sure Stream was okay. I had not been able to speak to her since I had been detained. Not knowing what had happened to her and the rest of my group was my greatest worry. My second reason was that I hoped seeing my brand-new computer with a nearly empty hard drive would convince Mr. Park that I was telling the truth. Perhaps I would then be released before the rest of the files on the hard drive were translated from English into Korean.

To my surprise, Mr. Park agreed. "We will contact her. We know where she is," he said. Then he left the room.

A while later he returned. "She refused to hand the computer over to us without you telling her to do so," he said.

"May I speak to her over the phone?" I asked.

"No," he said. "Write her a letter telling her to cooperate."

I did as I was told. But instead of releasing the computer, Stream wrote me a letter of her own, which was handed to me just a couple of hours later.

"Kenneth," she wrote, "I was told to make a phone call to the hotel to give the authorities your computer, but I don't know if this request is from you or from them. To make sure this is you, answer this question: What is my ex-boyfriend's name?"

"Answer her and let's get this cleared up," Mr. Park said.

"Yes, of course," I said. I grabbed a pen and started to write the answer to her question, but I froze. The ex-boyfriend's name had completely escaped me. I remembered conversations with Stream about this man. She had dated him for a while.

Ten minutes passed. I knew the man's name. I could hear her say it. But for some reason I could not remember it.

Finally I wrote, "Stream, for some reason I cannot remember your ex-boyfriend's name. But here's something only you and I know. Our office is on the twenty-fourth floor. Rather than take the elevator, you usually go up and down the stairs to burn some calories."

My answer was enough for her, but it also worried her. She insisted she be allowed to speak to me on the phone. Again, to my surprise, the North Koreans agreed. Later that evening, I was able to call her on the phone.

"Kenneth," Stream said in a tone that sounded almost desperate, "why couldn't you remember something so easy? What are they doing to you?"

I became very emotional at the sound of her voice. Only a couple of days had gone by since I had seen her, but it felt much longer. "I am okay. Where are you? Are you safe?"

"Yes, yes, I am fine. No one else in the group has been arrested," she told me.

I felt a weight lift off my shoulders. "I am so glad. Please cooperate with the officials. Please call the hotel to release my laptop to the DPRK authorities so they can inspect it."

The tour group was scheduled to leave the next day, so I told her to leave the country along with them. She didn't want to. "I want to stay here with you. I don't want to leave you here by yourself."

"Stream," I replied, "you must leave with the group. I am your boss, and you must listen to me. Please contact the American consulate in Shenyang and let them know what is going on."

I finally convinced her to leave. In my mind, the best thing she could do for me was to get out of the country and out of the reach of any DPRK agents who might try to abduct her.

The DPRK agent in Yanji brought my laptop from the hotel safe back to Rason and gave it to the officials investigating my case. Neither Stream nor I ever saw the laptop again. I'd had it less than a week.

Later that same night Mr. Park returned. "Your computer checks out. We now believe you when you say you intended to transfer files from the hard drive to your new computer."

I was momentarily relieved. I shouldn't have been.

"However, we are far from finished in our investigation of you. The materials on your hard drive raise serious questions. You will remain here until we learn the answers, but your group can leave."

My hopes of release evaporated, but right then it did not matter. Everyone from my group was safe and on their way home.

When Mr. Park arrived for the fourth day of interrogation, he told me my group had crossed the border back into China that morning.

Thank you, Lord, I prayed. *Now I am free to tell the truth without endangering anyone else.*

Aloud I said, "I am ready to make a confession."

Mr. Park grinned. "Follow me," he said.

He led me to the living room of the suite. Three other officials sat in the chairs as if they had been waiting for me. I took a seat on a chair in the middle of the room that faced all four officials.

"I am ready to make a full confession," I said, which made everyone in the room happy. I took a deep breath and then said, "I am a missionary and a pastor. I brought tourists into the country to worship God, to pray on behalf of the North Korean people, and to show the love of Jesus Christ to the people of this land. My tour company was a front for my missionary work. That's who I am and what I have done."

"Why did you do this?" one official asked.

"All of Korea had once been on fire for the Lord. I wanted to bring in believers who would once again pray and worship in this place and for these people, but to do so privately, where the people living here would not see it."

I had kept everything a secret because I knew that if we tried to evangelize openly, we might endanger their lives as well as put ourselves at risk. But by coming into the country and demonstrating the gospel through our actions and interactions with the people who live here, we would pave the way for more sharing down the line.

I was neither the first nor the only missionary to serve this way. Many missionaries currently work in North Korea, and nearly all operate legitimate businesses, including bakeries, noodle factories, and clothing factories. These companies provide much-needed essentials as well as jobs to North Koreans while also allowing their owners and employees to show the gospel through their actions.

To the DPRK authorities, missionaries are terrorists—operatives sent by the CIA to infiltrate foreign countries and disrupt their societies. Once the missionaries do their job, the CIA can overthrow the legitimate government and set up a puppet controlled by America. Essentially, that is how North Korea views South Korea—as nothing more than a puppet state of the United States.

I knew the authorities would not understand what a missionary actually does, which was one of the reasons I was so reluctant to divulge the true nature of my work. The North Korean view of missionaries, and their negative view of Christians and Christianity, is why I brought in teams to pray and worship but not to do evangelism. I know it sounds odd to think of a missionary who doesn't tell people about Jesus, but I felt in my spirit that the time was not yet right for that.

Everyone in the room looked stunned, except Mr. Park. The corners of his mouth turned up just a little with a "Gotcha!" sort of smile.

"We know you are a missionary," he said in a condescending tone. "We have talked to many people about you. We found the mission letters on your hard drive. It is good you finally confessed, but we already know who you are."

Apparently they had translated enough of my English files to know the real nature of my work. Undeterred, I retorted, "Then you also know that I brought this hard drive in purely by accident. If I wanted to sneak something into the country, I would have brought in a small USB stick, not a whole hard drive."

"Yes, I know you made a mistake, a costly mistake. You accidentally brought in your battle plan, and now we have it. Now you must tell us where you got those video clips. Write down who made them and who had you bring them here."

I immediately noticed the change in Mr. Park's question. Before, he had asked why I had brought in these materials and what I planned to do with them. Now that I had admitted the true nature of my work, he wanted to know who the masterminds were behind my sinister plot.

"I have no idea. I haven't watched most of them," I said.

Mr. Park's expression flipped from good cop to bad cop once again. He clearly did not like my answer. "They are yours," he said with a firm but low tone. "You were going to put them on your new computer. How can you say you don't know anything about them?"

"The only one I have watched is the documentary by Lisa Ling." A couple of times I had used *Inside North Korea* as part of the orientation for outreach teams that came to Dandong to pray for North Korea without actually entering the country. The documentary follows Sanduk

Ruit, a Nepalese eye surgeon, as he operates on one thousand blind North Koreans hand-selected by Pyongyang. When the bandages come off, the people respond as if they are at a Pentecostal healing service. They jump up and down in disbelief. Tears of joy flow as these people who once were blind now can see. But instead of thanking the doctor for giving them sight, they fall down in front of the photograph of Kim Jong Il. Weeping, they cry out, "Thank you, Great Leader, for giving me sight! We love you, oh Great Leader."

"You say you haven't watched them, but you have them. Who gave you all these videos?" Mr. Park yelled.

"I got them years ago. Someone sent them to me long before I ever started coming into your country. I never even watched them. I forgot they were on my old computer," I tried to explain. "When I transferred files from my old laptop to the external hard drive, I copied all of them. I didn't go through each one."

"So you *do* remember who gave them to you." That sly, gotcha smile returned. "Now we are getting somewhere. Who gave them to you? Tell me his name. Where is he now?"

While it was true I had forgotten about the videos on my hard drive, I knew exactly who had given them to me. One of the missionaries on my team in Dandong, a South Korean named Mr. Wang, had given them to me a couple of years earlier. He and his wife went through one of our first Discipleship Training Schools in Dalian back in 2008. When I started the Dandong center, they came with me and joined the staff.

I really did not want to mention Mr. Wang by name, because that would put his life in danger. Koreans in Dandong are not out of the reach of DPRK agents. Many have been abducted there, and there's nothing that can be done to stop it. The last thing I wanted to do was put more people in jeopardy.

Instead, I told Mr. Park, "The man who gave me the videos was another missionary, Mr. Cho." Mr. Cho was a real person. He had gone through one of my earliest training schools and had worked at our base as a staff, but he had passed away that summer. Since he was dead, I used his identity for Mr. Wang.

Mr. Park smiled and nodded his head as if to say, "Finally the truth."

"But Mr. Cho died last summer of stomach cancer," I continued. "I am afraid he is dead."

"Are you sure he is dead?" Mr. Park asked. I could tell he did not believe me.

"Yes."

"I see," he said, skeptical.

I tried to hide my nervousness, but I don't think I did a very good job. I knew God was with me. He promised to stand beside me, but I was not worried about myself. The longer this questioning went on, the more names were going to come out, whether I said them or not. What then? What would the DPRK agents do to my friends and coworkers if they could get their hands on them? And what did the North Koreans plan to do to me?

THE POWER OF PRAYER

"If you believe, you will receive whatever you ask for in prayer."
—MATTHEW 21:22

MR. PARK STORMED INTO my room, angry. Up until his arrival my morning had been very pleasant. I started the day by filling the tub with hot water and soaking in the warmth. The guards made me get out after only five minutes, but for those five minutes I felt only peace.

After my usual small breakfast, the guards ordered me to sit in a chair. Sitting still was supposed to be punishment, but I used my time to meditate on God and worship him. With no phones or e-mails or anything else to distract me, I was able to focus on connecting with God in a way I never could in the outside world. I had been in custody for a week, and this time alone with God had turned my detention into a spiritual retreat.

My sense of peace flew out the window when Mr. Park burst into my room, his face even redder than usual.

"We know what you have been up to!" He spit the words at me.

"I told you," I replied. "I am a missionary." I did not understand why he was so upset. In all my seventeen previous trips, I had never given out one Bible or converted one North Korean person. I did not start an underground church or engage in any subversive activities. All

I had done was lead groups of people from North and South America, Europe, Africa, Australia, and Asia to worship and pray privately, just among ourselves.

"I came here because I love the people of North Korea, and I wanted to pray for them. Why does this upset you? You don't believe in God. Why should it matter to you if we pray to a God you don't believe is even there?" I said.

"We have a god," Mr. Park replied, "and his name is Kim Il Sung. You came here worshiping a different god, and that is a crime. And you say you came to pray for us, but I know you. Since you believe in a different god, you came to pray *against* us and *against* our Great Leader."

"How can this be so dangerous if my God does not exist?" I asked. I did my best to keep from smiling, but I found this conversation more than a little funny.

"Because you are just getting started. Your whole work is designed to undermine faith in our Great Leader and to destroy our country."

"How?"

Mr. Park shook his head. "You know how," he said in a low voice. "You come here with Westerners, with more Christians. And no matter what you say, they will talk. They will tell people about their god, and someone will believe their lies. The lies will infect our people like a virus, because it will spread from one person to two. Then those two will become ten, and the ten, twenty and thirty and a hundred, and then the hundred will become thousands, and more and more people will lose faith in the Great Leader. When that happens, our great nation will be destroyed, which is exactly why you have come here." He stopped and stared at me for a few moments.

Wow! I thought. *He really gets the power of prayer and the power of the gospel to transform an entire society. He gets it. They all get it. That's why they are so afraid. I'm not dangerous, but Jesus is.*

I thought back to my seminary classes in St. Louis, where professors tried to explain what happens when faith in Jesus really takes hold. I'm not sure most Christians understand it, but here, in the most isolated country on earth, the people in charge do. They know how powerful faith in Jesus is, and it scares them to death.

"So what do you have to say for yourself, Bae Junho?" Mr. Park asked.

"Nothing," I replied. Everything he said was true, with the exception of his inferring that bringing down the DPRK government was my ultimate goal. I came because God sent me to show people he loves them and has not forgotten them. That is all.

"'Nothing?' You will say more than nothing," Mr. Park said. "I want to know exactly what you have been up to the past six years. You will write out for me everything you did in both Dalian and Dandong. Tell me who sent you there, who you worked with, and all your activities. You moved to Dandong, just across the border from us. Why? Why didn't you stay in Dalian? There are many North Koreans in Dandong where you operated your training center. Give us the names of all the North Koreans you trained in your center." He then smiled his good-cop smile. "All I'm asking you to do is tell the truth. Please, no more lies. Just give me the information I need, and things will be much better for you."

Mr. Park left me alone at my desk with the familiar stack of paper and a new pen. My new writing assignment presented a much greater problem for me than any before. He wanted names, but I could not tell him all the names of the people involved in my work in Dalian or Dandong. At the same time I could hear the Lord speak to my heart, *Just tell the truth*. How could I tell the truth and protect my friends and family?

The story of my missionary work is not a story about me but a story of God's faithfulness. A year after I graduated from San Francisco Bible College, I moved my young family to St. Louis, where I attended Covenant Seminary. My family and I arrived in St. Louis with all of fifty dollars in my pocket. I didn't know how we were going to make it. Then God presented me with two jobs, one as a youth pastor and the other as a janitor at a Christian school. Beyond my work, I found a letter at my school mailbox not long after my first semester of classes started. Inside was fifty dollars and a note that said, "Dear Kenneth, I have been praying for you. The Lord told me to give you fifty dollars a month until you graduate, and that's what I am going to do." I still do not know the identity of the sender. It remains a mystery to this day.

After graduating from seminary I served in a variety of positions at several churches, including a one-year stint with a ministry in South Korea. In 2003 we moved back to the United States, where I served as children's pastor with a church in Georgia. But I resigned a year and a half later, when my marriage fell apart. I felt as if a giant boulder had fallen out of the sky and crushed me. When I realized my marriage could not be saved, I moved to Seattle and moved in with my mother. I had hit rock bottom.

One night I just broke. I was weeping over my family when the Lord spoke to me. *You are trying to seek your wife's heart,* he said, *but how about my heart? Seek me first and my righteousness, and I will add everything else unto you.*

Then God reminded me of a commitment I had made to him a long time ago. *I called you to China, and you said you would go, but you never have. You've been disobeying me all this time.*

This was a turning point for my life. I got up off my bed with the assurance that God's faithfulness never ends. I still felt broken, but I was ready to seek healing. That's how I ended up at Youth With A Mission's Kona campus for an extended Discipleship Training School. Even though I was a seminary graduate, the DTS showed me things about God's character and how much he loves me that I had somehow failed to grasp before.

The Discipleship Training School consists of two parts: an intense twelve weeks of teaching followed by the opportunity to go out and do what we were taught. That was how I ended up going to Dalian on the trip where I crossed the Yalu River to North Korea. A year later I returned to Dalian to visit and ended up staying there.

And that's what Mr. Park wanted to know about. He didn't care about my stories of God telling me to go to China or North Korea. All he wanted to know was who sent me and what I did when I arrived.

I pondered the "who" question for a while. Finally I wrote, "You asked who sent me to China and then ordered me to move to Dandong. The answer is God and his Son, Jesus Christ, through the Holy Spirit."

As for what I had done when I arrived in Dalian, the first thing was to work with a growing team to start what we called a J-House. The *J* stands for Jesus. This was a safe place where various outreach teams could stay inexpensively and worship and pray without worrying about any kind of government restrictions. We also provided food and networking for teams during their stay.

J-House was also a training center. We talked to the teams about how you cannot go out in the streets and start preaching. Nor can you force anyone to listen to what you have to say. Instead, we showed the teams the importance of building relationships with people. We started an English Corner at a coffee shop, where our teams of volunteers from around the world could get to know Chinese students. We focused on showing people God's love. If they asked why we had come to China, we told them. If they asked about God, we told them more about him as well.

Over time the English Corner grew into English language Bible studies, marriage seminars, and sports ministries. At the same time, I set up a cultural exchange business, which is how I was allowed to stay in China on a work visa. The cultural exchange program also gave a reason for all the activity in the J-House, since mission work was not officially allowed.

The real story for me is not what we did but what God did. When I went to look for a place to use as a J-House, I had all of $300. I needed a house large enough for the teams we hoped would come over. I looked at thirty-six apartments, most with three or four bedrooms. The Lord said, *Bigger.* Finally I found an eight-bedroom, four-bathroom house that could hold at least thirty people. It had a large room we could use for worship services and an attic we could turn into a prayer room.

The rent, however, was ¥180,000 a year, or $24,000, all of which had to be paid up front. I knew God wanted us to have this house, so I prayed, *If this is your house, and this is your will, this is your bill, Lord.* Since it was his bill, I also asked how much he wanted to pay. I heard ¥150,000, or $18,000.

I asked the owner, "Can you lower the rent to ¥150,000?" Then I added, "We can't pay all the money up front like you ask. Can I pay for the first two months now and pay every three months instead?"

She said no.

"If you change your mind, please give us a call," I replied. My team and I marched around the house every day for a week, praying to God, just like the Israelites had marched around the city of Jericho as described in the book of Joshua.

On the seventh day the owner of the house called. She agreed to lower the price to ¥150,000 a year and allow us to pay every three months. She asked for only two months' rent up front.

I shared the news with my team, and we all celebrated. Then I added, "I still have only $300, but we need $3,000 for two months' rent. We need to keep praying."

Right before we had to make the first rent payment, two donations arrived. God did not give us $3,000. No, he gave us $6,000, which gave us enough money to rent apartments for all the staff as well.

The first J-House set the tone for all my work in China. During my time in Dalian, I always asked visiting teams if they would like to see North Korea. Almost everyone did. I took them over to Dandong, four hours away. I took teams out on a boat to see North Korea on the other side of the Yalu, but I did not have them land on the other shore. My friends who rebuked me after I made that trip in 2005 were right. It was too dangerous to risk arrest for nothing but the privilege of saying we had touched North Korea. I kept my teams just offshore as we prayed for the country and the people trapped inside it. On that first trip on the river, I had asked God to use me as a bridge for North Korea to the outside world. This was my way of doing that. I wanted the visiting missionaries to see the country and start praying for it.

The work in Dalian kept growing. We saw many Chinese students and others come to Christ while I was there. We had so many that in January 2007 we put on a mini-DTS like the one I had attended in Kona. We promoted the school in local churches and arranged for teachers to come in, but we didn't have a place to hold it. The J-House was already full.

A couple of days before we were scheduled to start, one of our team members visited a local coffee shop called Starback Café (instead of Starbucks) that had a conference room above it. The team member started talking to the owner about Jesus, and the owner became a Christian. Twelve hours later he threw open his doors for us to hold our mini-DTS there. Twenty-six students came, some having traveled more than twenty-four hours by bus or train to get there.

We ended up holding English Corners at the café, along with worship services and all sorts of mission work, until we moved our work to Dandong in 2009.

A year later, in 2008, God sent eighteen students to the J-House for our first DTS, seven of whom were Chinese but spoke primarily Korean, six Chinese students who spoke Mandarin, four South Koreans, and one North Korean woman named Songyi. We were already taking a huge risk training Chinese students. If the government found out, I could have been kicked out of the country. To make matters worse, not long after the school started we discovered Songyi's visa had expired. If she were caught in our school, she would be deported and possibly face a very long prison term or even death.

We actually had a close call in the sixth week, when the police came by our center. As soon as they walked in, our Bible classes suddenly became English classes. Songyi hid underneath a bed until they left.

When the DTS was over, Songyi stayed with us for another six months. She moved with us when we shifted our center of operation from Dalian to Dandong. I felt God calling us to move our operation there because nearly every team that came to Dalian ended up going with me to Dandong to pray for North Korea from the opposite side of the Yalu River. Just as God had miraculously provided a place for us in Dalian, he did the same thing on an even larger scale in Dandong. Instead of a house, he gave us an entire hotel to use for our DTS. The new location also allowed us to reach more North Koreans because the city had a large population of North Korean workers.

A few months after the move to Dandong, Songyi decided to return to her home. Before she left she thanked us for all we had done. Then she told me she planned to start an orphanage in her hometown.

"There are so many street children in my town who need help," she said. "I want to shelter them and teach them what I have learned here."

That statement created a real problem. If she had merely wanted to start an orphanage, the DPRK government would have looked the other way. However, her desire to open a Christian orphanage, even an underground one, immediately put her at risk.

I did not mention Songyi in my answer to the question, "What did you do in China?" but Mr. Park found out about her anyway. After I finished writing, he returned to the room, took my work, and then left. About an hour later he came back with a photo printed from my hard drive. He pointed at a woman.

"Who is this? She is one of ours!" By this time he had read enough of the letters on my hard drive to know that one or more North Korean nationals received training at our center. "I know you trained her in China. Who is this woman, and where does she live?" he demanded.

My heart sank. I feared if he knew the truth about Songyi, her life would be in danger. Then I thought back to God's promise that no one would be harmed through this.

Okay, God. I trust you. I will tell him what he wants to know.

That's not exactly what I did, however.

"Her name is Songyi, but she lives outside of Pyongsong." I made the last part up.

Mr. Park seemed satisfied with my answer. He left the room but returned a short time later. His ears glowed red and veins popped in his neck.

"You are a liar, Bae Junho!" he screamed. "Don't you know we will find out the truth? *What is her real name and where does she live?* No lies this time."

I told him the whole truth while praying in my heart for her safety.

Mr. Park listened and then left with the paper on which I had been working when he had barged in with the photo of Songyi. I had told the truth. Now I had to hold on to God's promise: *No one will be harmed.*

A guard brought my lunch. After I ate, he said, "You may go to your bed now. We have been told to let you rest for a while."

I could not believe my ears. After days of round-the-clock interrogation, I could not believe they were going to let me rest in the middle of the day. It did not take long for me to go to sleep.

When I woke up, the guard ushered me back to the main room, where I was instructed to sit and wait for Mr. Park. Another official, one I had noticed since the beginning but with whom I had had very little contact, approached me.

"So you are a missionary," he said.

I nodded.

"Let me ask you a question. I have heard of God, but I have never heard of this Jesus. Tell me, in which village does he live? Does he live in North Korea or China?"

I looked at the man to try to tell if he was just kidding with me. He wasn't. This was a sincere question. He honestly wanted to know where Jesus lived and why I would take such a risk to come into a closed country to tell people about him.

Before I could answer, Mr. Park returned. He clearly did not like what I had written for him. But then again, he never did.

"You," he yelled to the other man. "Out!" The man did as he was told.

Then Mr. Park turned to me. "I want the truth." He tossed more papers at me. "Write," he demanded.

I did as I was told, only to have to rewrite my answers when Mr. Park hated what I had written. We did the same thing the next day. And the next. And the next. Day after day I wrote about God, and day after day Mr. Park yelled at me to tell him who had really sent me to China and Dandong and, ultimately, North Korea. I kept telling him the truth, but he never accepted it.

All the days started running together. I spent my mornings in the presence of God; then I spent my days writing and rewriting the same thing over and over and enduring the consequences for not getting it right. Mr. Park continued going from good cop to bad cop and back again. Through it all I continued to rely on the promise God made to me on the day when my hands grew warm and his presence felt so real. God was with me. He would bring me through this. And no harm would come to anyone. That's all I had to keep me going, but it was enough.

SIX ————————————————————————

OPERATION JERICHO

*When the trumpets sounded, the army shouted, and at the
sound of the trumpet, when the men gave a loud shout, the wall
collapsed; so everyone charged straight in, and they took the city.*

—JOSHUA 6:20

NIGHTS WERE HARD for me during the month I spent confined in Villa
Three. Whenever I first closed my eyes, I always saw my wife, Lydia,
and my children. I missed them so much. *Surely everyone knows what has
happened to me by now*, I told myself.

I wished I could pick up a phone, call my children, and explain the
situation myself. I knew they had to be very worried. If they could hear
my voice, then maybe they could relax a little.

I was also worried about my wife's safety. I hoped she had left
Dandong and had moved as far from the North Korean border as possible.

"Are you safe, Lydia?" I whispered in the night. "Are you safe?" The
worry was more than I could bear. But then I remembered God's promise.
No one will be harmed. He had not told me that *I* would not be harmed,
but that *no one* would be harmed. *The Lord will take care of her*, I reminded
myself. My worrying wasn't going to help him do his job any better.

I decided I needed to focus on what I could control. Given my circumstances, that was very, very little. About the only things in my control

were how I reacted to my captors and what I wrote for Mr. Park's assignments. I had to release everything else to God's hands.

Worrying about my family was a natural thing for me to do. However, if I had known how far the agents were in their translation of the English files on my hard drive, as well as the information they had learned from Songyi and the others they had interrogated, I would have been worried about what was going to happen to me next.

"What is Jericho?" Mr. Park asked as he barged into my room one morning.

I swallowed hard. *He knows*, I said to myself. I had dreaded this moment from the minute I realized the portable hard drive was in my briefcase, and now it was here.

"Jericho is a city in the Bible," I replied.

That thin, sly smile returned. "You know, I almost believed you. I almost believed you when you said you just brought people in to pray. But now I know there is more. You still haven't told me everything." He paused. "I ask you again, what is Jericho?"

"In the Bible, Jericho is a very old city where many of the Bible stories take place," I said. I knew what he was getting at, but I didn't want to volunteer any more information than I had to.

Mr. Park leaned back in his chair. "You had a good game plan, you know. A good operation." He paused to see my reaction. "So tell me, Bae Junho, what is *Operation* Jericho?"

I felt sick in the pit of my stomach. I had to choose my words very carefully. "Operation Jericho is what I call my plan to bring people into the country to pray. I told you about it when I confessed to being a missionary. The name comes from a Bible passage in the book of Joshua, where the Israelites marched around the city of Jericho and prayed."

"Here is your Bible," he said, handing it to me. It was the first time I had seen it since my arrest. "Write out this story exactly as it appears in your Bible. I want to read about this Jericho for myself."

I opened my English NIV Bible to Joshua 6 and wrote out the first twenty verses, which describe how the priests and Israel's army marched around the city every day for seven days, carrying the ark of the covenant with them. On the seventh day they marched around Jericho seven times; then they blew their trumpets, people shouted, and the walls came tumbling down. I stopped with verse 20. I did not think I needed to include verse 21, which says, "They devoted the city to the LORD and *destroyed with the sword every living thing in it*—men and women, young and old, cattle, sheep and donkeys" (emphasis added).

After I finished writing, Mr. Park grabbed the page and started reading. I had to wonder if this was the first time he had ever read anything from the Bible.

As he read, I could see his anger rise. By the time he got to the end, his whole body had started to shake. He dropped the paper and grabbed a large crystal ashtray that sat on the desk. Before I knew what was happening, he flung his arm as though he were going to throw the ashtray at my face.

I quickly threw up my arms to protect myself, but he did not let the ashtray fly.

"This was your plan all along!" he yelled. "You wanted to completely take over our city, didn't you? You plan on conquering Rason, and then what? Do you plan to take over all of our great nation?"

"No, no, no," I said, waving my hands. "You don't understand! Even though the verses in the book of Joshua describe an ancient battle, I used the name only because of how the people pray. I don't want to take over anything. Operation Jericho is not about literally taking over a city."

"Do not lie to me!" Mr. Park said in a threatening tone. "We know about the prayer center you planned to put in the heart of Rason." My jaw dropped. "Yes, that's right. Your friend Sam talked. He told us all about it."

Mr. Park misread my reaction. I was not shocked he had learned about my plan to rent a space in Rason where the teams I brought in could pray. No, I reacted out of fear for Sam. He was my friend who operated the coffee shop in the hotel where I had been arrested. Like Songyi, he had been discipled in YWAM, and he had just begun to serve at our center in Dandong. I knew they would try to interrogate him, but I had hoped he had been able to get out of the country before he was detained.

"But I never started anything," I said. "The prayer center was not for North Koreans. It was a place for the people I bring into the country to pray. And I never actually started it. It was just an idea. That's all."

"And you would do what you call *spiritual warfare* there?" Mr. Park added.

"Yes," I said. As soon as I said this, I wished I could take the word *warfare* back. Mr. Park jumped on it.

"We read about the spirits you say rule our great nation," he said. One of the documents on my hard drive was part of the presentation I made to every group before they came into North Korea. In it I talked about spiritual warfare and the seven spirits that I believe dominate the country.

"You call them the spirit of idolatry." He paused after each one. "The spirit of fear. The spirit of lies. The spirit of hatred. The spirit of division. The spirit of pride. The spirit of control."

He looked at me. It was the first time I thought I saw genuine hatred in his eyes.

"You call these spirits, but you are really talking about our government. This is how you really feel. The lies, the fear, the control—you say this about us. That is why you want us to be destroyed."

"I am sorry, I am sorry," I pleaded. "This is a misunderstanding. I did not mean to offend you. I apologize."

"You say this is a misunderstanding," Mr. Park said, suddenly switching to his good-cop persona. "Okay. Enlighten me. I want you to tell me all about Operation Jericho and explain to me how it is not a threat to our great nation." He pointed at the paper on the desk. "Write it out. Tell me all your Jericho plans." He turned to leave but stopped before he reached the door. "No lies this time. Tell me the truth."

Even before Mr. Park left the room, I started praying for wisdom. I needed God's guidance on how much of the Operation Jericho plan I should share.

I feel the same way now, three years later, as I write this chapter. As I mentioned, I was not the only undercover missionary working in Rason. Anything I divulge has the potential to endanger the lives of those trying to share the love of Christ in one of the most closed countries on earth.

The plan for Operation Jericho came to me in 2010, during my second trip into North Korea. I had returned to the country to explore the possibility of bringing tour groups there. One day I went for a walk on the grounds of the hotel where I was staying in Rason, sort of like the walk I was on when the agents in the black sedan showed up to arrest me.

As I walked across the hotel grounds, I felt the Lord say to me, *My people's eyes are blind. They cannot see. My people's ears are deaf. They cannot hear. My people's mouths are mute. They cannot speak. I will open their eyes so they will see my glory. I will open their ears; they will hear my voice. And I will open their mouths. They are going to praise my name and give glory to me. I will heal my people. I will redeem them. I will restore them.*

I remember not knowing what to say in response. I prayed, *Lord, I don't know what I can do.* Talking about God with a North Korean is illegal. I didn't know how I could possibly open their eyes.

I had already started working on a plan to bring in tour groups as a way of opening their eyes to the needs of the North Korean people. Now I realized I could do more than simply show them the need. I thought of Joshua and the walls of Jericho. Huge spiritual walls encircle North Korea. Jericho was the first city the children of Israel encountered when they went into the promised land; Rason is the first North Korean city open to outsiders.

The two thoughts went around in my head until I thought, *We can pray down these spiritual walls!* Our group in China had already prayer walked around multiple properties, and we saw how God answered those prayers, just as he answered the prayers of the priests walking around Jericho. *We can do the same thing for a whole city and an entire country, because this is God's idea. He wants to set these people free.*

When I returned to Dandong, I started brainstorming ideas that became the actual Operation Jericho. I wasn't concerned about juche or the political system or the Leader. Instead, I felt such a burden for the North Korean people that I wanted to do something for them. I thought back to the soldier who had come out of the darkness to ask me for money and cigarettes. What I really wanted to give him was the love of Jesus.

That was my underlying motive behind Operation Jericho. I wanted to take people into the country to love the North Korean people with the love of Jesus. These people live in such darkness. They know nothing of Jesus, but we have to show them Jesus before we can tell them about him. That's why prayer was at the center of Operation Jericho. As people pray, the spiritual walls around the country will come down, one brick at a time. I also wanted the people I brought into North Korea to experience the beauty of the country and its people, and to hear from the Lord directly while they were there, just as I did.

All Operation Jericho was ever meant to be was a plan to mobilize prayer warriors to intercede for the people of North Korea. That's what I wrote down for Mr. Park: "I love the people of North Korea, and I want to be a bridge for them to the outside world."

Unfortunately, when I first wrote out the specifics of my plan years earlier on my computer, I used metaphors that could easily be misunderstood by non-Christians, especially by the DPRK authorities. Within the Word document I used phrases like, "We will mobilize the Lord's army to bring down the wall," but I did not mean a literal army. I was talking about people all over the world getting down on their knees to pray for the people of North Korea.

Mr. Park did not see it that way.

When he read what I wrote out for him during our interrogation session, he exploded. He knew more than I dared mention, because he'd read the document on my hard drive—the one I never thought anyone but me would read.

"This is not the whole truth! This is not all of your plan. You plan to invade our great nation, claim it, and conquer it. Do not deny it! I have read these words that you wrote yourself." He got up and walked across the room. "You are a dangerous criminal, Mr. Bae. You came here intent on destroying our great nation, but you have been stopped. Now you are going to pay for what you have done."

I did not say anything. I thought it best to keep quiet.

"You have violated Article 60 of our constitution," he said. "This is a very serious crime. Perhaps the most serious. Do you know what the penalty is for violating Article 60, Mr. Bae?"

I shook my head.

"Death," he replied with a slight smile.

CONFESSION

Truly he is my rock and my salvation;
  he is my fortress, I will not be shaken.
My salvation and my honor depend on God;
  he is my mighty rock, my refuge.

—PSALM 62:6–7

OPERATION JERICHO WAS the last straw for Mr. Park. It confirmed all his suspicions about me. I had confessed to being a missionary, but now, because of Operation Jericho, he seemed convinced I was just the front man for a much bigger conspiracy.

"Who sent you here?" he demanded the next time he came to interrogate me.

"I told you. God called me here," I replied.

"Who sent you here?" he asked again as if he didn't hear me.

"God."

"Who sent you here?" he asked again, his patience wearing thin.

"I have tried to explain it to you. God spoke to me and called me to be a bridge to North Korea," I said.

"Do not lie to me!" he yelled. "Do you think I am a fool? Do you think I cannot figure out who is really behind all of this? We have been patient with you, but our patience has limits."

"I understand," I said, "but I have told you that I am just a missionary."

"Do not say you are just a missionary anymore," Mr. Park said in a soft voice. His personality had swung back to the good cop. "We know you work for YWAM. There is someone over you there, right?"

"Yes," I said. "His name is John, and he oversees the work in Dandong."

"And who is above John?" Mr. Park asked.

"I guess that would be Loren Cunningham, the man who started Youth With A Mission," I said.

"Now we're getting somewhere. And above Loren Cunningham is Obama. That's who sent you to our country to terrorize us and bring us down. So you must actually work for the CIA. Obama and the CIA are behind this," Mr. Park said.

I did not know what to say to such strange logic.

"You deserve to die for what you have done," he continued. "First, you have dishonored our Great Leader's name with your anti-DPRK materials. For that alone you deserve to die. Second, you conducted your Operation Jericho, twisted the minds of North Korean people, and sent them back into our great nation as missionaries working against us. You have attempted to overthrow our government through prayer and worship and bringing in outsiders. The penalty must be death, or perhaps a life sentence. But no lower than that."

"Okay," I said.

That set Mr. Park off. "What? You don't care that you may die for your crimes? We don't even have to wait for a trial. If we wanted we could just take you out right now and chop off your head and be done with you. Human life is worth less than a fly's here."

"You know what? Do whatever you want," I said. I wasn't trying to be brave. I had just had enough. I was too tired to go on with this farce. For four weeks I had endured Mr. Park's questioning from 8:00 a.m. to 11:00 p.m. every day. I had taken about as much as I could endure. If they wanted to kill me, so be it.

"Do not threaten me, Mr. Bae. Don't you realize your life is in our hands?" Mr. Park replied.

"My life is in God's hands," I said. "You say you might kill me. Don't you know that will just make me a martyr? That is the highest honor that a missionary can ask for."

I thought to myself, *You have no idea who you are dealing with. I am an ambassador of the most high God. God sent me here. He is still in control, no matter what.*

Mr. Park blinked at me. He didn't know what to say. I had never talked to him like this. I don't think anyone ever had.

I expected another angry tirade. Instead, Mr. Park responded with silence. After a few awkward moments he got up and left the room.

Later in the evening, Mr. Park returned. "I have good news for you," he said. "You are going to Pyongyang, and you will get to go home from there."

Now I was really confused. A couple of hours earlier, he was threatening to chop off my head and dump my body out in some remote corner of the country. Now he was telling me I may get to go home soon. I let out a slight groan. "How?"

The look on his face told me he had been waiting for this moment. "Even though you have committed such a serious crime, you have behaved and cooperated with us. There may be something our government can do for you."

"What do you want me to do? What do I need to say to go home?" I was ready to do anything.

"If you confess to what you have done, and if you offer a sincere apology for your crimes, our government may well show you mercy," he said.

"So what do I have to say?" I asked.

"Now these must be in your own words," he said.

"Yes, I understand," I said. "But what am I supposed to say? Just tell me what you want me to write down that will get me home, and I will do it."

Over the next hour or so, Mr. Park told me different things to write, and I wrote them down. "Confess how you attempted to overthrow the government with prayer," he told me. I also had to include details about Operation Jericho, about how I had trained North Korean people as disciples of Jesus, and about how one of these people came back to start a Christian orphanage. Of course, I also had to confess my crime of disrespecting the leadership of the DPRK.

I wrote what I thought Mr. Park and everyone else behind the scenes wanted to read. I believed that if I confessed to everything they had accused me of doing, they would finally let me go home.

After I wrote my confession, Mr. Park took it and left for a very long time. Eventually he returned with a paper in his hand. "We took the liberty of writing your confession for you," he said.

"Okay," I replied. "Do I just sign it?"

"No, no, no, of course not," he said in a way that made it sound like I had just suggested something completely absurd. "The confession needs to be in your words and your handwriting. Take this and rewrite it to make it your own. But make sure you include everything in it. Do not leave a single word out."

I sighed. How was I supposed to do that? I grabbed a pen and started on my assignment. As best I can remember I wrote:

I, Kenneth Junho Bae, violated the law of the DPRK (Democratic People's Republic of Korea) by attempting to overthrow the government by the means of prayer and worship. Using my mission work as a cover, I served as an instrument of an American imperialistic devious attempt to take over the nation by corroborating anti-North Korea propaganda and supporting the crushing isolation policies of the United States and South Korea. I brought in more than three hundred Christian intercessors from over seventeen countries to the DPRK, disguised them as tourists, and had them pray, worship, and love the people of the DPRK with the love of Jesus Christ. Under a plan named the Jericho Project, I purposely reached out to the Christian communities around the world to come, pray, worship, and love the people and claim the land of North Korea for God. By doing so, I believed that just as the walls of Jericho fell, the wall around the city of Rason would fall.

I also attempted to set up a prayer center in Rason using the Rajin Hotel as a base. Although the purpose and the usage of the building were strictly for the foreigners, I confess that by setting up the prayer center in DPRK, it had a major impact and influence in the city of Rason.

By having Christian tourists come and demonstrate the love of Jesus Christ through their actions, such as smiles and acts of good will, I tried to influence the people of the DPRK to turn toward God rather than the government or the leadership of the DPRK. I acknowledge and confess that these actions were taken to break the unity of the people of the DPRK by trying to influence them with Christianity. I acknowledge that my actions seriously violated the law of the DPRK.

I confess that I set up the prayer centers and training bases in China to mobilize, train, pray with, and send missionaries to the DPRK. Over six years, I have conducted seminars, orientations, and prayer meetings for more than eight hundred people from dozens of nations to pray for North Korea.

I also want to acknowledge and confess that I have seriously disrespected the leadership of the DPRK, and I want to apologize for my crimes of disrespecting and spreading false rumors regarding the leadership. Through my learning from the Western media, and from the anticommunist education that I received in South Korea, I spoke against the leadership to the North Korean nationals in China. I said things such as "What kind of leader would allow more than three million people to starve to death in the twenty-first century in prosperous East Asia?" and "Water flows from upstream to down. Water from upstream needs to be pure in order for the downstream water to be clean." I realize that by saying these remarks to North Korean nationals, I tried to blame the DPRK leadership for the suffering of the people, thereby breaking the trust and the loyalty of the people to the leadership.

I also confess that I trained North Korean nationals with Christian discipleship training, and I sent a North Korean back to start a private orphanage in North Korea. I attempted to influence the children of the DPRK to love God rather than the Supreme Leader. Through this action, I acknowledge that children will grow up knowing the love of God and drift away from the love of the Father, the Leader of the nation. I understand that if ten children come to believe in Christianity, they will eventually turn into larger numbers, and it will break the unity of the nation that is united together with the Leader. Setting up a private orphanage run by North Korean Christians could seriously jeopardize the security and unity of the people.

I realize that my actions have seriously violated and disrespected the leadership and the government of the DPRK, and I want to apologize and ask for forgiveness for my wrongdoings.

Signed,

Kenneth Junho Bae

Mr. Park smiled when he read my confession. "Yes, yes, this is exactly what we needed. Now we also need you to write out your apology."

This was not the first time I was told to write a formal apology. I had written multiple versions already as part of all the other things I had to write for Mr. Park. However, if he wanted a new apology letter, and if it would get me home, then I would apologize again.

"Do you have specific things I need to apologize for?" I asked.

"Why of course," he said, as if we were old friends. After listening to him rattle off his list, I wrote something very close to the following:

1. I apologize for disrespecting the leadership of the DPRK.
2. I apologize for trying to bring Christians to North Korea to pray, worship, and love the people of North Korea through the love of Jesus Christ.

3. I apologize for bringing a hard drive that contained anti-DPRK videos clips, although it was purely a mistake.

4. I apologize for disguising as a tour guide when I am actually a missionary and a pastor.

5. I apologize for trying to set up a prayer center in Rason, although it was strictly for the foreign tourists.

6. I apologize for training North Korean nationals with spiritual Christian training.

7. I apologize for the attempt to set up a private Christian orphanage in the DPRK and trying to influence the children with the love of God instead of the love of the Leader of the DPRK.

8. I apologize for setting up the bases in China to conduct seminars, orientations, and trainings for North Korea.

9. I apologize for trying to mobilize, train, and send missionaries into the DPRK.

10. I apologize for not speaking the truth from the beginning.

I handed my finished apology to Mr. Park. He was clearly very pleased as he read it. "This will do. This will do nicely."

I wish I could say I was relieved, but I wasn't. I just wanted to go home. I would be relieved when they finally released me.

Mr. Park left. A guard came in and told me I could lie down and rest for a while. I collapsed on my bed and fell asleep. When the guard woke me, he had me return to my chair to wait. I didn't know what to expect, but I was hoping for some good news.

Later in the evening, a second guard came in. "Stand up," he ordered.

I stood up as the bujang from my first day of detainment walked into the room. After spending a month surrounded by very thin, small people, I thought he looked even larger than before. He had some papers in his hand.

The bujang took the seat across from me and waved his hand at me, telling me to sit down. He laid the papers on the desk. It was my signed confession.

"You have confessed to a very serious crime. Do you understand? You have violated Article 60 of our constitution, and for that you face *jooktang*."

The word *jooktang* is difficult to translate into English. South Koreans never use the word; only North Koreans do. It kind of means, "You are the scum of the earth, and we are going to beat you to death and completely destroy you." Basically, it is a death sentence carried out with a joyful vengeance.

"However," he continued, "you have been very cooperative, and you have behaved yourself so far. Of course we will take all of that into consideration." He smiled, but his smile did not reassure me. To me it felt like the smile a cat gives a mouse right before eating it. "Other people want to see you now, people in Pyongyang. We know there is more you have to tell us, but those in Pyongyang want you, so we are going to send you there."

"When?" I asked. Since we were close to the border where this situation had started, I had assumed they would send me back the way I came and tell me never to return. Now the bujang was talking about sending me to Pyongyang.

Whatever, I thought. *I'll make a side trip to Pyongyang before I go home. Then I will get to see my wife and everyone else. With any luck I will be home for Christmas.*

The thought of going home excited me. I had not stepped a foot out of this suite, much less gone outside, since my walk in the hotel parking lot a month earlier.

"Tomorrow," he said. "When you get there, cooperate with the investigators. If you do, everything will be fine for you. Just listen to them and do what they tell you to do." With that, he stood up and walked out of the room.

A short time later Mr. Park returned. For the first time I was actually glad to see him. "You told me that if I confessed, I would get to go home," I said.

"Yes," he replied.

"But they are sending me to Pyongyang tomorrow."

"Yes," he said in a way that sounded like, "Of course. What's the problem?"

"So why are they sending me to Pyongyang, and how long will I be there?" I asked.

"You are going there to meet with the federal authorities. They want to verify the answers you gave us here. It will not take long," he said.

"How long?" I asked again.

"Not long. Perhaps a month," he replied.

"And then I will get to go home," I said.

"As long as you keep your story straight," he replied.

After Mr. Park left I spent the rest of the evening getting my things together and preparing to finally leave the room that had been my prison for a month. Although I had not seen most of my possessions since my arrest, the Rason officials let me have some of my clothes so that I had something to wear during the interrogation period. As I packed my bags, Mr. Park walked in and handed me a piece of paper.

"What's this?" I asked.

"Why, your bill, of course," he said.

"My bill? For what?"

"Your room and your food."

I read through the bill very quickly. At the bottom it said, "Total: ¥20,000," which is about $3,000. I'd brought about ¥1,300 into the country with me to cover taxis and other small expenses my group would incur during our four-day stay. But this was ridiculous.

"I don't have this kind of money," I said.

"Perhaps you can contact your wife and have her bring it to you," he said.

As much as I wanted to talk to my wife, having her bring me money was the last thing I would have ever done, even if I had the money lying around at home. I wanted to keep her as far from North Korea as possible.

"I can call her and ask her to wire the money here," I said, hoping that at least she could hear my voice and worry less about me.

"No, I don't think so. No phone calls for you," Mr. Park said on his way out the door. Another official came into the room to further discuss the bill with me. After much back-and-forth with this official, another man who must have been a little higher up in authority came in and told me not to worry about paying the bill. "We'll just add it to the expenses you will incur in Pyongyang."

"Fine. That will be great," I said. If it would have gotten me out of the country, I would have found a way to raise the money. I just wanted to go home, and the sooner the better.

The very thought of my ordeal finally ending made me too excited to fall asleep. I was going to go home to my family. I couldn't imagine how worried they must be because I had not been able to contact them during the entire investigation. But now I was going to Pyongyang for a short stay, and then I was going home!

Little did I know, the worst was yet to come.

EIGHT

ON TO PYONGYANG

"The Lord is my helper; I will not be afraid.
What can mere mortals do to me?"

—HEBREWS 13:6

I THOUGHT I was on my way home when I left Rason. I knew I had to go to Pyongyang first, but I believed it was just a formality. In my first month of detention, keeping track of time was difficult, because I never got to go outside. Every day felt exactly like every other day. But by listening to the officials and the guards in and around my room, I was able to tell I had been in custody exactly one month. They had detained me on November 3. That meant it was now the first week of December.

The trip to Pyongyang started early. A little before six o'clock, Mr. Park came to my room and said, "Let's go." He escorted me outside to a waiting Toyota Land Cruiser. Another man, who I assumed also worked for the same government agency, stood next to the car, waiting for us.

"Get in," Mr. Park said, opening the back door for me. I climbed in. The other man got in the car on one side of me; Mr. Park sat on the other. Just as in my car ride to the Bipa Hotel, I was once again stuck in the middle of the backseat. Thankfully, the Land Cruiser was much roomier than the Chinese compact car the first agents drove.

Two other men approached the car. Before they got in, Mr. Park warned me, "Do not say anything about your case in front of these men. They do not work with us. They are local Rason officials who also have business in Pyongyang. They're basically just along for the ride."

I nodded in agreement.

One of the two men got in behind the wheel to drive us. The other sat in the front passenger seat. Mr. Park bowed slightly to him and said, "Good morning, sir. Thank you for coming with us today."

In the DPRK, the language you use shows the importance of the person with whom you are speaking. The respect Mr. Park showed told me that this man must be a high-ranking official. Later I found out that he used to be a deputy director of the international trade department of Rason.

As the two men climbed in the car, they stared at me in a way that made me feel a little like a zoo exhibit. Neither man seemed threatened by me or appeared at all hateful or angry at me. Instead, they both just looked curious.

"All right, let's get going," the official on my left said once everyone was in the car. The driver started the engine, and we were on our way. The sun had not yet come up when we pulled out of the hotel parking lot.

We headed south out of Rason. No sooner had we left the city than the roads turned to gravel. Rason is a major city and a key economic center of northeast North Korea, yet the highway that goes to Chongjin, the third largest city in the country, and then to Hamhung, an industrial and manufacturing hub and the second-largest city in North Korea, is nothing more than an unpaved country road, the kind one might expect to find in only the most rural, remote parts of America. Here, it passed for a major highway.

We had not driven far when the eastern sky began to brighten. The sun broke from the horizon over the Pacific Ocean. The important man in the front passenger seat smiled and pointed. "Wow, look at that sunrise," he said.

I didn't know how Mr. Park and the other official in the backseat might react. My only other car ride with DPRK officials was quite tense. Not this one. Mr. Park and the other official in the backseat both looked and oohed and aahed over the sunrise.

"Beautiful," Mr. Park said.

I leaned up and looked out the window. It was the most beautiful sight I had seen in a long time. *Something to remember before I leave the country*, I thought.

We drove a little farther. The driver turned and asked, "Does anyone mind if I turn on the radio?"

"Please do," Mr. Park said. North Korean pop music filled the car. Mr. Park started singing along. I had never seen this side of him.

More surprises followed. At one point in the middle of the day, Mr. Park pulled out his phone and started watching a North Korean martial arts action movie. He held out his phone toward me. "Do you want to watch with me?" he asked. This did not seem like the man who had threatened to have my head chopped off.

After we passed through the city of Chongjin, the gravel road climbed up the mountains near the coast. Every once in a while, the Land Cruiser bounced and jumped from the big holes in the road. The road became quite narrow in places. I saw the remains of trucks and cars that had gone off the road and plunged down the mountainside. I prayed to God for safety, and I thanked him that our driver rarely got the car over thirty miles per hour.

The drive down the gravel highway turned out to be a real blessing for me. I had always wanted to see rural North Korea and the homes of average people. Now I got my chance.

Most of the houses were built by the government, which is another way Pyongyang keeps the people dependent on the Leader. Almost all the houses had the same cookie-cutter look. They were made out of concrete instead of traditional building materials. Most were painted white or sky blue.

Throughout the drive I noticed the men in the front seat kept turning around to have a look at me. Eventually their curiosity got the best of them. The official in the passenger seat asked a few questions about the cost of living in America. He had spent a lot of time in China because of his position, he explained, so he knew what life was like outside of the DPRK.

When we stopped for lunch at a seafood restaurant, the man who had been sitting in the front passenger seat said to me, "Mr. Bae, what would you like to eat? You can order anything that you like." He pointed at the crab on the menu. "How about some crab, or maybe some shrimp?"

I had trouble believing he was sincere. I had been told that I was the most dangerous criminal since the Korean War, and now this man wanted to buy me lunch.

"You know, I think I will just have soup with pork," I said.

Mr. Park shook his head but didn't say anything. He ordered the same thing as I did. The front seat passenger wasn't so shy. He ordered several dishes and shared them with the rest of us. Mr. Park and I ate well even though we did not order seafood.

When the man paid the bill, he used Chinese yuan rather than the DPRK currency. In Rason, where people have access to euros, Chinese yuans, and even American dollars, no one wants to accept North Korean money because its value constantly drops in the exchange rates.

As we walked out to the car, the front seat passenger laughed and said, "We all ate very well for less than one hundred yuan. This same meal would have cost us at least twice as much in Rason." One hundred yuan comes out to around fifteen dollars.

We drove several more hours after lunch. The sun went down, and we kept on driving. Finally, around nine or ten at night we reached Hamhung. The city is known for being an industrial and manufacturing hub, but it is also famous for Majon Beach.

As we got close to the city, the passenger in front turned and asked me, "Where do you prefer to sleep, near the beach or the city center?"

"I prefer the beach," I replied.

"Sure. I'll arrange it," the man said. He made a phone call and then announced, "We've got a place."

Before we headed for the hotel by the beach, the driver looked for a gas station to fill up the car for the next day's drive. We pulled into a few stations on the main road, but they either were closed or would not sell us gas because our driver wanted to use a gas ration card instead of cash. He finally found a place that agreed to accept his ration card. However, the electricity was out. The female attendant said she had to first turn on the generator before the pump would work, but the manager had just gone home and she didn't have a key to the storage room where the generator was located. "I'll call him and have him come back to turn it on," she said.

"How long will that take?" the driver asked.

"Not long," she said. "He doesn't live far away."

She made the call, but the manager never showed up. We sat in the car, waiting. After half an hour she came over to us. "Well, I guess he is not coming back. I will do what I can so you can get gas now." She disappeared for a few minutes and returned with an ax. I could not believe what happened next. She took the ax and started chopping away at the storage room lock.

I told everyone in the car, "This is really what is called *Hamnam spirit*." (*Hamnam* is short for Hamgyong Namdo, the province of which Hamhung is the capital.) This was a popular figure of speech for the can-do attitude of this part of the country.

Everyone laughed. Mr. Park asked, "How did you hear about Hamnam spirit?"

I smiled and said, "I know a little more than the average tourist."

After spending an hour trying to get gas, we finally left and headed to the hotel. The beach hotel took us about another half an hour out of our way. The fact that no one minded surprised me. The two agents who hauled me to the Bipa Hotel would never have gone for such a detour.

When we arrived at the hotel, we pulled up to a big metal gate. The guard asked us who we were and where we had come from. Then he asked, "Who does the car belong to?" He wasn't asking which of us owned the car but what branch of the government owned it. In North Korea, only the government owns cars.

"National Security Bureau," the driver answered. That's when I knew for sure that Mr. Park, the bujang, and all the other officials with whom I had dealt in the past month were all part of the NSB, which is the DPRK equivalent of the FBI and the NSA.

The hotel had a few villas, each with multiple rooms. Mr. Park and I stayed in one on the first floor. The other men in our group stayed upstairs. No sooner did we get to our room than Mr. Park said, "Why didn't you order something nice today at lunch when they offered to buy it for you?"

"I'm a criminal. How can I ask for crab or shrimp from the menu?" I said, only half kidding.

"You should have asked, and then I could have eaten it," he said. That's when I realized that eating out was a rare treat for him.

The rest of the evening Mr. Park seemed like a different man from the one I had known during my interrogation. He spoke to me as though I were a friend. When we got settled, he lay down on the bed and said, "I hate being gone like this. My little girl misses me so much when I am away. It's hard leaving her."

"How old is she?" I asked.

"Seven. You have children, don't you?"

"Yes," I replied. "Three."

"Are they over here or back in America?" he asked.

"Two are in America, and one is with her mother in our home in China," I said.

Mr. Park shook his head. "I don't know how you can be so far away from them."

We talked like this for a little while. Finally I had to ask, "How can you be so relaxed with me now?"

"What do you mean?"

"You aren't pressing me for information. You haven't asked me about my crimes. You are treating me like a friend."

"Why shouldn't I be relaxed? You've confessed to everything. I don't have to try to extract any more information from you. Plus, I realized you aren't a bad guy. You did what you did because you were deceived by all the misinformation you received in school in South Korea and through the media in America. Your religion also misguided you. I know you were sincere and thought you were doing good. You aren't a bad person; you've just been brainwashed with a lot of bad information."

I just smiled at him. I didn't know what to say in response. Over the next two years I would learn how ironic his statement really was.

When morning came I made a simple request: "I would like to go down to the beach before we leave." Our hotel was near the beach but not right on it. I had heard stories of how pretty this beach is, and it was one of the places I hoped to visit if I was granted permission to expand my tours. Now that I was actually here, I thought this might be my only chance to see it.

To my surprise, Mr. Park said, "Sure, why not?"

Mr. Park and I went down on the sand and watched the sun come up over the ocean. Even though it was December, the air temperature was not that cold. It was one of the prettiest sunrises I've ever seen, even more beautiful than the one the day before.

Once the sun was up we headed inland, driving straight west toward Pyongyang. The road wasn't much better than the one we had traveled the day before. Snow started falling, which slowed us down. The snow showed me a side of North Korea I can hardly believe exists.

In most cold-climate countries, snowplows keep roads clear in winter. That is not the North Korean way. Instead, I witnessed ordinary people all along the highway pushing snow off the road by hand with snow shovels, as if they were cleaning their driveways. I even saw young mothers, with their babies on their backs, out shoveling snow.

"What is going on?" I asked.

Mr. Park seemed surprised. "What do you mean?"

"All these people out on the road shoveling snow. Where do they all come from?"

"They live around here," he said in a tone of voice that made me feel like I had asked a crazy question.

"But why are they shoveling the road?" I asked.

"To clear the snow. When it snows, everyone must pitch in to keep the roads open. That is part of what makes our system great. We all work together and rely on one another. No one is exempt. That's why you see mothers with children as well as doctors and even party officials out here. We all must do our part," Mr. Park said with a bit of pride in his voice.

"Don't they have jobs?"

"Yes, but the common good comes first. They come out and shovel before they go to work." Mr. Park looked out the window at the line of workers with shovels. He smiled at them as we drove past. "What do they do in America, let the snow pile up?"

"No, we have snowplows that clear the road for everyone," I said.

He shook his head with the kind of look a carpenter gives someone trying to drive a nail with the heel of a shoe. For the next few hours we drove past tens of thousands of people with snow shovels clearing the highway all the way to Pyongyang, a distance of nearly two hundred miles.

The road improved when we got closer to Pyongyang. Eventually we reached one of the few paved highways in the country. It still did not compare to the highways in the United States or South Korea. The constant snow made its condition even worse.

The drive took two or three times longer than it might have taken in America. I wished we could have driven as fast as on an American highway, because I was ready to get this ordeal over with. The faster we arrived in Pyongyang, the faster I could answer the last round of questions and go home. On my third day of detainment in Villa Three, I had felt the Holy Spirit's presence and God's promise to bring me through. Now I felt as if the finish line were finally in sight. It could not come soon enough for me.

The mood in the car remained light. Music played. A couple of hours out from Pyongyang, Mr. Park pulled up a video on his phone of a comedy club in Pyongyang. The segment made fun of President George W. Bush's IQ and his looks. Everyone in the car laughed and laughed as the actor had Bush make all kinds of silly commands that made it look like America could be brought down very easily. The video used a couple of clips and music from an American movie that also made fun of President Bush. The video was actually pretty funny, but I felt very awkward laughing at one of our presidents while sitting in a car full of people who hate our country. However, I did not make a big deal of it, because I figured everyone needs to laugh sometimes—even in North Korea.

After the video the man in the front passenger seat peppered me with more questions about what America is really like. Mr. Park even said, "I never knew some of the things you told me about how people talk about the DPRK in the West. No wonder you think the way you do."

A few miles outside of Pyongyang, our car slowed down in the middle of the highway. There aren't many cars in the entire country, so I didn't think we were in a traffic jam. I looked up ahead and noticed a black North Korean–made SUV stopped in the middle of the road. Two men in dark suits stood next to the car. Our driver came to a complete stop and rolled down his window. One of the men from the other car walked over to the window and looked back at me.

"Okay," he said to our driver, "you follow us." The man went back to his car and escorted us into the city.

I turned to Mr. Park. "How long again do you think I will be here?" I guess I needed a little reassurance.

"Maybe a month at the most. Don't worry about it," he said with a smile. "Just stick with your story and cooperate, and you will be fine."

I hoped he was right.

We exited the highway and drove into the heart of Pyongyang. The car in front led us down several streets before slowing down in front of a restaurant. Our driver pulled our car right behind it. The two cars then turned into a narrow alley behind the restaurant that came to a dead end at a large metal gate. The gate opened, revealing a very ordinary two-story building that could not be seen from the street. We pulled through the gate and parked in front of the building. The two men from the front car came back to our car and looked at me. One of them said, "Come with us."

Mr. Park opened the door, climbed out, and let me out. That was the last I ever saw of him.

I was led through the front door. Inside looked like a clubhouse to me. It did not look or feel like a police station or a prison. The two men led me further down the hall, past several doors, to a downstairs room. "In there," one said. I walked in and found a hotel-type room with a desk, a couple of chairs, and a television, along with a twin bed.

One of the security officials said, "Make yourself at home and relax. Lie down if you like, or you can even watch some TV. If you need anything, just let us know." He turned and left.

I looked around. No one was standing guard, at least not in my room or immediately in the hall. However, I knew they were watching me. On the wall there was a security camera that could see the entire room.

The drive had left me very tired. I lay down and immediately fell asleep. Later I woke up and flipped on the television. It didn't take long to go through all the channels because there was only one to choose from. The news was on. Every story was about the beloved Supreme Leader, Kim Jong Un.

When the news broadcast ended, the channel did not go to commercial. Instead, the scene shifted to a concert. A woman in a tight-fitting military-type uniform was singing before a packed house. The song seemed to be an intense love song. Tears filled her eyes. I thought, *Wow, this is a very emotional song for her.* Then I listened closely to the words. I'd never heard a love song like this. She wasn't singing about a man.

No, she was singing of her love for the Supreme Leader! I would have changed channels, but this was my only choice.

After the music video a movie came on. *Good*, I thought. *I love movies, and I haven't seen one in a very long time.* My enthusiasm was short-lived. The movie was about Kim Il Sung, the original Great Leader, as he led troops into battle against the Japanese in World War II.

I turned off the television and went to bed.

The DPRK officials pretty much left me alone for those first three or four days, although I noticed guards had been posted at my door. I slept most of the day, trying to make up for the fatigue caused by a solid month of intense investigation. When I was awake, I explored my room. Inside one of the desk drawers I found the words *Love Nest* scrawled in English. I suspected I wasn't the first American prisoner detained here. I later learned that almost every American detained through the years had stayed in this same compound.

When I wasn't looking for secret messages, I slept as much as I wanted, watched television when the channel was actually broadcasting (which was only a few hours a day), and read. They gave me back my Bible right after I arrived in Pyongyang. I had not had it during the month in Rason, and I had missed it terribly. Some days I read it for eight hours or more.

Nearly every day the electricity cut out for an hour or two, sometimes longer. I had come to expect that. From my experience on previous trips, I had learned to always take the stairs in multistory buildings, even when my hotel room was on the sixth or seventh floor. There are few things worse than getting stuck in an elevator during a prolonged power outage.

Overall, those first few days in Pyongyang allowed me to rest and regain my strength. I assumed officials were going through my testimony and questioning Mr. Park so that they could verify everything I had written in Rason. Once they finished, I expected to be sent home.

That's all I wanted—to go home. God had sustained me through my month of captivity in Rason. In spite of the death threats hurled at me, I knew God was going to protect me, and he did. The prospect of going home had made the previous month seem more bearable. Now I had stories to tell. I even held out hope that I might get to resume my work in North Korea, or, at the very least, back in China.

On my fourth day in Pyongyang, I was sleeping in my bed after lunch when a man burst through my door. I jumped up.

"Please sit down," the man said. He looked to be about my age, in his midforties. He was thin but taller than the average North Korean. "My name is Lee Chul, and I am from the supreme prosecutor's office," he said, introducing himself. "It took me a while to get up here to see you myself because there was so much information to go through. Mr. Park was quite meticulous."

"You talked with him?" I asked.

"Of course. We've talked many times over the past four days."

I was relieved. If they had talked, then surely they had discussed my release.

"Bae Junho, I am here to inform you that as of today you have been officially charged with crimes against the Democratic People's Republic of Korea. Your government has been notified of the charges against you. Today marks the beginning of the pretrial proceedings."

I shook my head in disbelief. "Trial?" I asked. I was so taken aback by the word that I did not ask why the United States government only now had been notified of my situation. I was led to believe that they had been contacted right after I was first detained.

"Yes. Trial. During the pretrial period we will verify all the information you gave Mr. Park in Rason. Just because you said something doesn't make it true. We will question witnesses and investigate your case thoroughly. Once we are ready, you will stand trial."

I could not believe my ears. "I'm going to be tried, as in go to court and be formally prosecuted?"

"Yes. Of course. What did you think was going to happen to you?"

"I . . . uh . . . ." I didn't know what to say.

"Mr. Park told me you have cooperated in the past. If you continue to do that, then everything should go well for you. I am sure you will have a good result."

I didn't ask what a good result might be. I hoped he meant I would go home, but it didn't sound like I was going home any time soon. "How long will that be?"

"As long as it takes," he replied.

FAR FROM HOME

I love you, LORD, my strength.

The LORD is my rock, my fortress and my deliverer;
*   my God is my rock, in whom I take refuge,*
*   my shield and the horn of my salvation, my stronghold.*
— PSALM 18:1–2

I WAS ACTUALLY excited the first time I was allowed to watch television in the Pyongyang detention center. After weeks of no music, no movies, and no books or magazines, I welcomed the break from the silence. For me and for most every American, television is entertainment. Not in North Korea.

I quickly learned my captors were not "letting" me watch television. As part of my reeducation program, I *had* to watch it every day from the time the central channel began broadcasting—around five in the evening—until it went off the air at ten thirty. Later in the evening a second channel started broadcasting, with a third that came on, only on the weekends, but they weren't much better. The government uses television as a propaganda tool to shape the minds of the North Korean people. My captors hoped to shape my mind as well.

Every day one of the four guards assigned to me came into my room at five o'clock and told me to turn on the set. (The four guards rotated their shifts, changing every three hours, twenty-four hours a day, seven days a week.) I had no choice but to obey. On the days I turned the set off early, a guard immediately came in and ordered me to turn it back on.

The television was the best and worst part of my day. It was the best because it broke up the monotony of sitting in a solitary, silent room. But it was the worst because of the nonstop propaganda I had to endure.

I can recall almost every line from the shows I watched because they aired the exact same show over and over for days at a time. Every day for a week they might show the same documentary of Kim Il Sung's rise to power. By the third or fourth repeat, I prayed for a power outage.

I once made the mistake of switching the channel in the middle of the Kim Il Sung movie. "What are you doing?" the guard stepped in and said. I explained to him that I had already seen this documentary four times.

"I do not care," he snapped. "You watch."

One weekend evening I turned on the central channel with a sense of dread. I could not take another movie about Kim Il Sung or Kim Jong Il. To my great surprise, a film started that appeared to be a drama about a family in the countryside.

Finally, something new, I thought.

I soon learned a lesson about North Korean moviemaking: no matter the genre—action film, love story, or crime drama—every movie ends the same way. The Great Leader, Dear Leader, or Supreme Leader always steps in and solves everyone's problems. This is the consistent message North Korean people hear from the moment they come into the world: The Leader is all you will ever need. He loves you. He cares for you. He will provide you with whatever you need.

Worse than the movies were the music videos that filled the time between programs. Most featured music from North Korea's number one pop group, the all-girl group called the Moranbong Band. Kim Jong Un himself handpicked the girls for their looks as much as for their musical abilities. I could not turn on the television without coming across their music videos. Every night I was forced to listen to songs with lyrics like,

> Today, tomorrow, always, I will stand next to him.
> Until the end, I will share my destiny with him. That is the
>   confession of my heart.
> Our comrade Kim Jong Un, our heart is being pulled to him
>   because of his leadership.
> Until my life ceases, I will never change my heart.

That was their hit song, "Confession." Another of their most popular songs is called "Burning Desire." The song kicks off with these lines:

> As we think about the Marshal who will go to a long distance
>   at this late night,
> Our hearts sincerely follow along his steps.
> Since our destiny, our happiness depends on the Marshal, our
>   only desire is the Marshal's well-being.

The Marshal is Kim Jong Un. His grandfather, the original Great Leader, Kim Il Sung, is the President, while Kim Jong Il, the son of Kim Il Sung and father of Kim Jong Un, is the General.

"Burning Desire" also included the line, "Because of the Marshal, our future has no limits." One night while I was watching this music video, the power shut off the moment after that line, and the television, along with the entire compound, went dark.

I laughed. "Yes, your future has no limits, but you can't keep the lights on," I whispered to myself.

I heard these songs so many times that the lyrics got stuck in my head. I found myself singing them without even realizing I was doing it. No matter how hard I tried, I couldn't get the lyrics out of my head. But then I thought about the words. It hit me: the songs weren't so bad. All

I had to do was remove the word *Marshal* and replace it with *Jesus,* and the songs made great worship songs that we could even sing at church. I walked around singing the new versions. The more I sang them, the more I enjoyed them. I doubt if the Moranbong Band or Kim Jong Un would have felt the same way about my changes to their lyrics.

Besides giving me new songs to sing, the constant propaganda barrage helped me understand how ordinary North Koreans feel about their leader. I tried to imagine what it would have been like for me to have been born here, which is what would have happened to me if my grandfather had not escaped during the Korean War. If I had been born here and had seen and heard and been taught all this stuff every day for my entire life, I would be praising the Supreme Leader as well.

I came away with much more compassion and understanding for the North Korean people. The world where Kim Il Sung is god is the only reality they know. No wonder they found me to be such a threat.

The impact of the constant propaganda campaign was most obvious in the news programs. Every story reminded the viewers that North Korea is paradise on earth. According to their media, the DPRK is the envy of every country on earth. Newscasts also pick up wire feeds of stories from America and the West. North Korean newscasts show every video of shootings, street riots, and acts of violence in America, along with footage of every wildfire and hurricane and tornado and flood. Basically, they show anything and everything that makes America look bad. From watching the news night after night I came to understand that people here sincerely believe America is nothing but poverty and violence and death.

On December 12 the television broadcast started earlier than usual. As always, I had no choice but to watch. As soon as the television came on, I saw a very excited newswoman in a pink traditional dress. She almost bounced out of her seat with excitement.

"We have successfully launched the Kwangmyŏngsŏng 3 satellite aboard a Unha 3 rocket!" she said in a way that reminded me of Walter Cronkite announcing Neil Armstrong and Buzz Aldrin landing on the moon. "I repeat," she said, "we have successfully launched the Kwangmyŏngsŏng 3 satellite aboard a Unha 3 rocket!"

The newscast then switched to scenes of people celebrating in the streets of Pyongyang. Many cried for joy. Some danced while most just walked about almost in shock, like a little kid who finds a pony next to the tree on Christmas morning. To them, this news was almost too good to be true.

I did not have the same reaction. "This isn't good," I said as I stared at the television. Pyongyang had tried several times to launch a satellite but had never succeeded, although they always claimed that they were successful. All the previous attempts had been condemned by the United States and most of the rest of the world as nothing more than a concerted effort to develop an intercontinental ballistic missile capable of reaching the United States. This situation is very serious because the DPRK also has nuclear weapons.

I knew that if North Korea truly had put a satellite into orbit— and you never can really believe anything you see on North Korean television—they now had a way of dropping nuclear weapons on the West Coast of the United States. Pyongyang had already threatened to use nukes against America. I don't think they really will, but to the people of the DPRK, the Korean War never officially ended. Both sides reached a truce, but a formal peace treaty has never been signed.

When I put all this together, for me—sitting all alone on the other side of the world, held prisoner by a country that hates my home and blames it for every evil North Korea has ever suffered—December 12, 2012, was not a good day.

I started to lose hope. I had not received any mail from home, nor had I heard anything that might lead me to believe the United States government was working to rescue me. Even though I had twice been told that the US State Department had been notified of my detention, I doubted that they had. If they did know about me, I could not understand why they did not appear to have taken any kind of action. Now, after the missile launch, I wondered if they could even if they wanted to.

North Korea tells its people that the United States started the Korean War when it invaded the North. America is considered to be a continuous threat, which makes engaging in any kind of negotiations—even over something as small as an American missionary who mistakenly carried an external hard drive into the country—really, really complicated.

I later learned that the State Department had publicly acknowledged the fact of my detainment only the day before, on December 11, 2012. My guess is that the overlap of these dates was not a mere coincidence but a part of the larger North Korean political strategy.

The celebration in the streets was still on the television, but I ignored it. I wanted to turn off the television, or at least turn off the sound, but I knew the guards would not let me. I did my best to shut out the noise as I sat in my room, thinking about my situation. My mood sank. Depression set in.

Then I remembered all the giants in the Bible who also ended up in jail unjustly. I thought about Joseph. I could really relate to him. First, his brothers sold him into slavery. Then he ended up in prison because his owner's wife lied and accused him of attempted rape after she failed to seduce him. Joseph's family had pretty much assumed he was dead. No one remembered him in that jail. But the Lord "was with Joseph and gave him success in whatever he did" (Genesis 39:23).

I sensed God whisper to me, *Remember, I am still with you.*

I opened my Bible to the psalms, whose prayers carried me through many dark days. Flipping along I came to Psalm 91. The words leaped off the page at me, especially the last few lines. While people danced in the streets of Pyongyang, celebrating the launch of a rocket that might one day be able to deliver nuclear weapons as far away as California, I read:

> "Because he loves me," says the LORD, "I will rescue him;
>> I will protect him, for he acknowledges my name.
> He will call on me, and I will answer him;

I will be with him in trouble,
I will deliver him and honor him." (vv. 14–15)

I read these verses over and over. I heard God repeating these promises to me. *I will rescue you, Kenneth. I will protect you. I will answer you. I will be with you in trouble. I will deliver you and honor you!*

Joy washed over me. I thought about the charges against me. The DPRK had accused me of planning to start a prayer house in Pyongyang. Since I had already been charged, I might as well make good on it.

"God, this is your house!" I proclaimed out loud.

The guards heard me. If Mr. Lee was nearby, he had to have heard me too. Anyone on my floor of the detention center must have heard me. I didn't care.

"Oh Lord, you love these people. You want to restore your people back to you, so I lift them to you. Draw them to yourself, O Lord."

The more I prayed out loud, the more I felt the Spirit of God moving within me. I mixed in praise songs with my prayers. I looked around my room. "O God, I give this room to you. This room is your place. This is holy ground, O Father! And on this holy ground I stand. I will not move. I will not retreat. I will not stop declaring your praises. I will stand with you no matter what! I will hold my ground!"

The guard at the door glanced in at me. The expression on his face suggested he thought I was crazy, but he also looked a little frightened. He didn't say a word but just went back to his post.

The Spirit filled the room as I continued to pray aloud. "My enemies surround me, Father, but I will not give way, and I will not give in. O Lord, open their eyes. Show them your glory." Suddenly thoughts of the 1907 Pyongyang revival filled my head. "Do it again, O Lord! Restore this land. Do again the work you did before. Turn the hearts of these people back to you."

A vision came to me: Kim Il Sung Square, in the middle of Pyongyang, filled with North Korean people worshiping and praising the one true God. "Oh, make it so, Lord!" I cried. "Oh, make it so!" What had started as a terrible day turned into one of the greatest moments of worship I have ever experienced in my life.

꿈

In the days after the satellite launch, the North Korean media increased its anti-American rhetoric. The government released a statement condemning the United Nations for hitting them with more sanctions; in the government's words, "The DPRK has a perfectly legitimate right to advance our space program." They went on to blame America for the sanctions. North Korea blames everything on America, even the fact that there are two Koreas.

(Guards and other officials told me, "If America would just leave us alone, all of Korea could come together under the Supreme Leader." I tried to explain how different South Korea is, including the large number of Christians there and how South Koreans have a freedom no one in the North has. "No one is going to want to give that up," I said, but no one believed me. They so firmly believed in the greatness of the Supreme Leader and the superiority of their juche system that they could not comprehend anyone not wanting to embrace it.)

Not only did I hear more anti-American rhetoric on television, but I also noticed my four guards' attitudes toward me were changing. At first they treated me a lot like the guards in Rason did. I was just a prisoner under investigation, nothing more. However, it didn't take long for my guards to start looking at me as though I were nothing but a filthy pile of scum.

It didn't help that the December temperature kept dropping. My room had heat, but the hallway where the guards had to stand did not. Twice a week a guard had to escort me to the sauna on the other side of the building, where I took a real bath and washed the few clothes I had with me. I always thanked the guards and tried to smile at them to show them I was not a threat. My attempted kindness did not help. The more times I went to the sauna, the angrier the guards became.

I think they also resented the fact that I was fed well, at least by North Korean standards. As I have mentioned, food is not abundant in the country. While I lost a lot of weight during my time in pretrial custody, I was not on starvation rations in Pyongyang. I think the guards resented that. They weren't yet openly hostile to me, but I sensed growing animosity.

The growing anti-American mood in Pyongyang made me leery of the prosecutors assigned to my case. I had met three so far. The first, Mr. Lee, was the man who had told me on my fourth day in Pyongyang that I had been formally charged. He had returned the next day with two other men. One introduced himself as the chief prosecutor. He explained how I was going to go to trial and how he, along with Mr. Lee and the other man, were going to bring the charges against me.

While the chief prosecutor spoke, Mr. Lee stood to one side, and the other man stood farther back still. The other man was older than Mr. Lee, perhaps in his midfifties, but much shorter. He didn't look like a happy man. Once the chief prosecutor finished his explanation, he and the second man left, leaving me alone with Mr. Lee.

Mr. Lee then became the primary prosecutor of my case. In the beginning he seemed pleasant enough. On the first formal day of the pretrial process, he explained how his job was to verify everything I had written during my time in Rason. This was no small job, because I had written about three hundred pages by the time they took me to Pyongyang.

"We have also brought in people for questioning to verify your accounts. And we have had investigators check out the people and places you talked about to make sure those all check out as well," he explained.

All of this struck me as strange because the officials in Rason had pretty much told me exactly what they wanted me to write down. When I didn't write it exactly like they wanted, they wrote it for me.

I asked, "Am I going to have to write everything out for you again and again, like I did in Rason?"

Mr. Lee waved his hands and smiled, "No, no. That's all finished," he said. "You have given us everything we need. I just want to go over it with you. Now, on the first day of your confession you said . . ." We spent the next couple of hours going over that page. He'd read off a line, and I had to say, "Yes, that's what happened."

We did this every day. He went line by line through my testimony, and I confirmed what I had written. He assured me that if I cooperated, things would go well, which meant I would go home. I held on to this hope, but at the same time, Mr. Lee often mentioned my upcoming trial. *How can I go home if I go to trial?* I wondered.

Also, the more of my confession Mr. Lee read out loud, the worse the guards' attitudes toward me became. When they heard what I had done, they went from treating me like an ordinary criminal to treating me like an enemy of the state.

After the missile launch, I expected Mr. Lee to start treating me badly as well. Thankfully, he maintained his same gentle tone. The way he asked his questions made me feel as though he were more my attorney than a prosecutor. He told me if I ever needed anything to just ask.

One day, a few weeks into the pretrial process, I said something to him about wishing I had a piece of candy to keep nearby because of my diabetes. "When my blood sugar drops, I really need to have some candy to bring it back up quickly," I told him. The next day, one of the guards brought me two bags. One was filled with all kinds of candy and chocolates, while the other had several two-liter bottles of soda. The guard had a scowl on his face. He was angry I received special treatment and enjoyed treats he probably could not afford.

Mr. Lee either didn't notice the guards' attitudes or didn't care. When he came to see me later that day, he said, "If you need anything else, you just let me know." I thanked him. He did things like this for me more than once.

A couple of weeks later, at the end of a session, Mr. Lee leaned back in his chair and gave me a once-over with his eyes. Then he smiled and said, "You know, you and I are about the same age."

"Yes," I said.

"I have to tell you that from everything I've learned about you, I can see you are the kind of guy who doesn't need the law to make you do the right thing. I know you came to our great country because you wanted to do some good. You aren't a bad person."

"I am glad you think that," I said. I kept my guard up. Even though Mr. Lee had done much for me, I could never be certain of his motives. He was the one prosecuting my case, after all.

"I am serious," he said. "You seem very sincere. Your ideas about right and wrong are just off, that's all. The teachers you had in South Korea filled your head with a lot of misinformation about communism and our country. And then you lived in the United States, where the twisted Western media spreads so many lies about us. They say our government let three million people starve to death at the beginning of the century, and you think, *What kind of government would do that?* So you come here to try to help people, and part of that is you tell people the stories you were told are true. I can understand that. But that stuff never happened. It's all lies.

"I can tell you are not really a bad guy," he concluded. "You are actually a missionary, not a CIA operative. I think you deserve a chance."

I thanked him for what he said. In the growing anti-American environment in which I now found myself, these were very bold words from a prosecuting attorney.

"I think you deserve a chance," he had said. I started to believe that he might actually try to make that happen.

TEN ————————————————————

FIRST CONTACT

"Whoever serves me must follow me; and where I am, my servant also will be. My Father will honor the one who serves me."

—JOHN 12:26

A FEW DAYS before Christmas, Mr. Lee came into my room with paper and a pen. "I would like you to write letters to your family," he said. "You have a wife, yes?"

I nodded.

"And you have extended family as well? A sister. Mother and father. Children, correct?"

"Yes," I said. "Can I write all of them?"

"No, just your wife, mother, and sister for now."

"How will they get my letters?"

"I can take care of that. Do not worry," Mr. Lee replied.

I wasn't sure whether I should believe him. As far as I knew, this might be another way of extracting information from me.

"Your letters cannot be long. You must urge your family to petition your government to do something to bring you home," Mr. Lee said.

"I will do my best," I replied. Since my arrest, I had replayed in my head conversations I wanted to have with my wife and family. Every night, when I tried to sleep, I thought about all the things I needed to tell them. I knew I couldn't pour all those thoughts and concerns into the letters I had been asked to write. My stories would never get past the official DPRK censors that I knew were going to read my letters before they sent them on to my family. If they even sent them.

I reminded myself that I didn't have to say much. *They just want to know I am alive and well*, I told myself. So that's what I told them. "Please do not worry about me," I wrote. "I am in trouble because I brought people into the country to pray for the people of North Korea, but I have been treated well. I am okay. God is with me. Please contact the State Department and ask them to help me come home."

All the letters had this same message. I added personal touches for my wife and also gave a longer reassurance that I was okay for my mother. Moms worry in a way no one else can.

Mr. Lee took the letters and placed them into a large manila envelope.

The next day, which I believe was December 21, Mr. Lee came into my room with two guards. "Please, come with us," he said.

I didn't ask where we were going. I had learned not to ask too many questions. Mr. Lee led me outside to a small minivan. Black curtains covered the windows. One of the guards opened the side door. He climbed in and slid to the far side. "You next," the other guard said. I climbed in, and the second guard got in next to me and shut the door. Once again I was stuck in the middle of a very small seat.

"Put your head down between your knees," a guard said. I did as I was told.

Then I heard Mr. Lee say, "All right, let's go."

The van traveled about ten minutes. We made a few turns along with a few stops and starts, which told me we were still in the city. When the van came to a full stop, the guard on my right opened the door and grabbed my arm.

"We're here," he said. "Get out."

Even though I was not supposed to know where I was, I immediately recognized the building in front of me as the Yanggakdo Hotel. It sits on an island in the Taedong River that runs through the heart of Pyongyang. The hotel is very popular with Russian and Chinese tourists. I had visited it on one of my earlier trips as a possible place for my tour groups to stay when I got the green light to expand my tours to the city.

Mr. Lee told the uniformed guards to stay in the car. He then led me inside the hotel. The doorman was expecting us.

"Good morning," he said to Mr. Lee. "Take the stairs there on the right."

Mr. Lee and I followed his directions. Once we reached the third floor, Mr. Lee took me to one of the hotel conference rooms. A couple of officials were waiting for us near the door. I guessed that they might be from the foreign affairs department. I was told to sit and wait.

After a few minutes two Western men walked into the room. "Mr. Bae," a blond, athletic-looking man said to me in accented English. He looked to be around forty. We shook hands as he introduced himself. "I am Karl-Olof Andersson, the Swedish ambassador to the DPRK. This is my secretary, John Svensson," he said, motioning toward a larger man about six feet tall and more than two hundred pounds. "Please, have a seat," the ambassador said.

Mr. Lee and I took our seats across from the ambassador. One of the two DPRK officials that had met us at the door had already sat down. I noticed he was writing down everything that was said.

"We have only a few minutes," the ambassador began, "so I have to be quick. We are here representing the United States' interests. I want to assure you that the United States government has been notified of your situation and is doing everything in its power to secure your release. Since your government does not have diplomatic relations with the DPRK, the US State Department will communicate with Pyongyang through our office. Your family will also be able to reach you through us. Also, until all of this is resolved, we will check in on you and monitor how you are being treated."

"Thank you," I said. I was relieved to know that someone outside North Korea actually knew about my situation and cared about me.

"How have they treated you so far, Mr. Bae?" the ambassador asked.

I glanced across at the man from the foreign affairs office, who was rapidly taking notes. Then I looked over at Mr. Lee. I wasn't sure how much English he understood.

"My treatment has been okay," I said. "I have not been physically mistreated or anything like that."

"Did they tell you why you are being held?" he asked.

"They have charged me with conducting a smear campaign against the country's leadership and with setting up mission bases in China to overthrow the North Korean government. They have also charged me with bringing people into the country to pray," I said. The ambassador wrote all this down. I then said something I probably shouldn't have said. "They also objected to things I said about North Korea in my orientation sessions for the tourists I brought in."

"How so?" the ambassador asked.

"I told people that North Korea attacked the South and that's what started the Korean War."

The ambassador just nodded and said, "Okay. Is there anything you would like to say to the US government?"

"I'm standing strong now, but I need their help. I need them to step in and do something so that I can go home."

The ambassador gave me a reassuring smile. "I understand," he said. "I know they are doing all they can right now. All right, I have another couple of things to address in the short time we have left. First, I have a privacy waiver I need you to sign. It authorizes us to release information about your situation. You need to check who we can give this information to. There are boxes for your family and friends, as well as the general population through the media."

I checked the boxes for family and friends. I did not want the media to become involved, nor did I want total strangers knowing about my being held. Deep down I still believed the misunderstanding that led to my arrest could be cleared up fairly easily. Until it was, I wanted to draw as little attention as possible to myself or the North Korean government. As crazy as it now sounds, I still held out hope that I could resume my work and bring tour groups back into North Korea. I thought that by showing respect for the North Korean government and by not embarrassing them in the media, we could go back to the way things were before.

"And last but not least," the ambassador said, "I have letters from your family." He pulled out a manila envelope and handed it across to me. I had never seen anything so wonderful in my life. "Your wife also wanted us to give these to you." He gave me a package that contained some warm shirts and a new pair of shoes. "I understand you have something for us," he said.

I looked over at Mr. Lee. He handed Mr. Andersson the letters I had written the day before. "Yes, please, if you would send these to my family, I would very much appreciate it," I said.

"Of course," the ambassador said. "If you need anything, have the DPRK officials contact our office, and I will see what I can do." Mr. Andersson and his secretary then stood to leave. I thanked them for coming and turned my attention to my letters.

Mr. Lee also stood. "You can read your letters first," he said as he and the other official left the conference room, leaving me alone.

I ripped open the large envelope and dumped out the letters on the table. My heart soared. I grabbed the letter from my wife and read, "My yeobo," she wrote, using the Korean word for "darling," "I am so worried about you. I waited three weeks before I wrote this letter, because I thought you would already be home. Stream told me what happened. She also informed me that the DPRK officials assured her that you were going to meet her at the customs office when she left the country. I keep waiting for you to come home. Where do they have you now?

"The first snows have fallen in Dandong. When you left, you did not pack for cold weather. I am so worried you are cold. Have they given you the medicines you need? I wish I could bring you your diabetes medication. I pray they have provided this for you. Your mother is holding up well. Your reputation is good in North Korea, so we hope you are treated decently while they clear up this misunderstanding.

"Please do not worry about us or the ministry here in Dandong. I will carry on the work until you return. No matter how long it takes I am here, waiting for you. I love you. Lydia."

I wept as I read her letter. I reread it several times. I could hear her voice. It was almost as though she were in the conference room with me. But at the same time, hearing from her made the distance between us seem so much greater, and it made me miss her so much more. I had never felt so far from home.

My mother and sister also sent letters to me. I wept as I read those as well. Both asked where I was. They tried to sound confident in their hope that I would come home soon, but I could tell both were very worried about me. They asked about my medications and whether or not I had seen a doctor.

"Why are they holding you?" my mother asked. She did not understand what was happening to me.

I'm causing them so much pain, I cried.

The conference room door opened. I assumed it was time to go back to the detention center. "Stay seated," Mr. Lee said. "To show you how humanely we treat even those who commit crimes against us, I am going to let you call your family."

"Now?" I said, my heart racing.

"Yes. Right now. You may call whomever you would like. Now, the purpose of the call is for you to inform them of the seriousness of your crime and to let them know that you are facing a trial for very specific charges. You must tell them exactly what the charges are against you. Here," he said, "take this paper and write down exactly what you are going to say based on what I just told you."

"Everything?" I asked. How could I possibly write down everything I was going to say? I didn't know what was going to come out of my mouth when I heard my wife's voice for the first time in two months.

"As close as you can. It is clear your family does not know how serious the charges are against you. They call this a misunderstanding. This is far more than a misunderstanding." Mr. Lee had clearly read my letters from home. Many people probably had. "You have to say, 'I am charged with violating Article 60 of the constitution, which carries with it the highest maximum penalty.'"

I did not want to say "highest maximum penalty," because I knew the words were code for the death penalty or life in prison. The phrase would further upset my family. But, of course, I had no choice.

"Okay," I said.

I scribbled out a basic outline of what I was going to say and slid it across the table. Mr. Lee gave it a quick read. Then he retrieved the telephone for me. "Who first?" he asked.

"My wife."

He dialed the number and handed me the receiver. My heart beat in my chest. But the call failed.

"May I try?" I asked.

Mr. Lee nodded.

I redialed the number. This time the call went through. The phone rang. Then I heard Lydia's voice.

"Hello," she said.

"Lydia. It's me, Kenneth."

She burst into tears. I also began to weep. I tried to keep to the script I had written for Mr. Lee, but it was so hard. I told her the charges against me, and I included the maximum penalty line, because Mr. Lee was standing right next to me.

"But do not worry too much about this," I reassured her. "Everything will be all right."

"How do you know?" she asked, crying.

"God has promised me I will not be harmed," I said.

I tried to say more, but Mr. Lee stepped toward me. "Time," he said.

"I have to go. I love you. I will be home soon," I said.

I then called my mother and my sister in Washington. Both calls were filled with tears.

"Please keep this as quiet as you can," I said. "I don't want a lot of publicity."

After I hung up, Mr. Lee escorted me out of the room, down the stairs, and to the lobby of the hotel.

I looked around. *I was just here a couple of months ago*, I thought. *I stood right here, in this lobby, a free man. Now I am a hated American criminal on his way back to jail.*

Christmas was four days away. The thought of spending it in the detention center sickened me. I wished I could turn back the clock. The sight of the lobby only made this feeling stronger.

Once I was back at the detention center, I read the letters from home over and over again. I tried to stay strong, but I could not stop the tears from rolling down my cheeks. In the six years I'd lived and worked in China, I had never once missed a Christmas with my family. I always flew home to the United States in time to celebrate with my children and spend time with my mother and sister. But not this year. I felt like the worst father and husband and son and brother in the world.

When Christmas Eve morning arrived, I remembered an idea I had had on my previous trip to Pyongyang, a few months before that fateful eighteenth trip. Back then I still enjoyed the officials' favor as a respected businessman who brought much-needed tourist dollars into the country. I had stayed at the Koryo Hotel, the finest and most famous hotel in Pyongyang. It was not far from the hotel I had just left. One evening I had looked out at the city from my window. Even though I had already led many prayer teams into the area around Rason, I still wanted to find a way to actually reach all the North Korean people, to show them that God is real and that he loves them.

It's hard to make a difference from a distance, I had thought to myself. Then a lightbulb came on. *Maybe I could actually live here for a couple of years. Yes, I could stay in Pyongyang for a year or two and maybe even have a special tour to celebrate Christmas in the capital. That might do it!*

"Well, you got your wish," I told myself. "Now what?"

I thought about this for a moment. I had wanted to bring people into the capital to celebrate Christmas, so I figured the least I could do was celebrate on my own. Sitting on my bed, I started singing Christmas carols, one after another. The more I sang, the better I felt. I kept on singing and singing and singing. It didn't really matter whether I was home in the United States or sitting alone in a North Korean detention center. Christmas celebrates Christ coming to earth, and that's what I was going to do. One of the names of Christ, Immanuel, means "God with us." I experienced Immanuel as I sang. God came near.

I sang all through the day. At five o'clock the guards told me to turn on the television. I was surprised by what I saw. It seemed the entire country was celebrating too. Then I remembered December 24 is treated as a national holiday in North Korea that celebrates the birthday of Kim Jong Suk, the wife of Kim Il Sung and the mother of Kim Jong Il. The movie of the day showed her as a freedom fighter, standing alongside Kim Il Sung as she mowed down Japanese soldiers with her gun. The movie made her out to be an action hero—like a real-life Black Widow from the Avengers movies, but more graceful and charming.

The movie played on the television while parties celebrating her life and the Great Leader went on around Pyongyang. I couldn't help but notice the irony. They celebrated the birth of their leader while I celebrated the birth of mine. I started singing "Silent Night" loud enough to drown out the noise of the television.

ELEVEN

Out for Blood

"Blessed are you when people insult you, persecute you and falsely say all kinds of evil against you because of me."
—Matthew 5:11

THE HOLIDAYS CAME and went. When I had left Rason, I had thought I would be home before Christmas. Instead, I was still in Pyongyang, waiting. My hopes rose when a newscast showed that Bill Richardson, former ambassador to the United Nations, was in North Korea, along with Google chairman Eric Schmidt.

This is it, I thought. *This is how these things always end, with a high-ranking or former high-ranking US official negotiating a deal.* But I never got to see Ambassador Richardson. Later I learned he personally carried over a letter from my son, which I received through the Swedish embassy a couple of weeks later. I assumed that Ambassador Richardson had pleaded for my release, but I was no closer to going home.

After having my hopes dashed following Ambassador Richardson's visit, I made a calendar to count down the days until I would go home. I set the count at thirty. *There's no way I will be here more than another month*, I told myself. *God won't leave me here like that, will he?*

Psalm 34:22 promises, "The Lord will rescue his servants." I prayed every day that God would rescue me, and quickly. Mr. Lee seemed to indicate that the government planned to send me home with nothing but a stern rebuke once he verified everything I'd written down during my month of detention in Rason. I prayed God would make it happen.

My hopes evaporated on February 12, 2013, when North Korea detonated a nuclear device in an underground test. This was North Korea's third successful test of a nuclear device. The United Nations immediately condemned the DPRK's nuclear program and issued more sanctions. Even China and Russia, North Korea's closest allies, spoke out against the test.

North Korea did not react well to the sanctions. Newscasts talked as though war with the United States were about to break out, and everyone seemed to believe it.

"America is a bully," one news anchor said, "but now we will stand up to him. Now he will not dare invade us." People interviewed in the street said things like, "America launches its own satellites and has thousands of nuclear weapons. Why can't we have one? This is not fair!" I heard people yell at the camera, "We're gonna nuke you if you guys don't leave us alone!"

I could tell they meant it.

The anger and hatred in the detention center increased as well. The chief prosecutor came to see me with a new threat. "You know," he said, "people are very upset about America. They are out for blood. What do you think would happen if they knew we had an American criminal here?"

"I don't know," I replied.

"Angry crowds would storm this place and kill you, and we wouldn't be able to protect you," he said. "People would stab you and cut you into pieces, and no one would stop them."

The guards' hostility grew more and more open every day. They made no secret of how tired they were of me. I overheard one asking the chief prosecutor why they were even bothering with me. "Why is he even here?" he asked. "He should already be in a labor camp or be put to death." I got the distinct feeling that any one of them would gladly volunteer to carry out the latter sentence. I was glad none of them carried guns. But then again, they didn't need guns to take me out.

The increased tension within the detention center was made worse by the disappearance of Mr. Lee. Without explanation, he just didn't show up one morning. Instead, the third prosecutor came into my room. I had learned his name was Mr. Min, which is pronounced "mean." The name fit him.

I stood when he came into my room, just as I was supposed to do. I even bowed in deference to him, which I also had been instructed to do whenever an official came into my room. Mr. Min just glared at me before he dismissively waved his hand at me to sit down. He pulled out a stack of papers, which I assumed was my confession and the other papers I had written in Rason.

Glancing over them, he shook his head in disgust. "You know what?" he said. "I don't buy it."

"Buy what?" I asked.

"Your story. I don't buy you saying you are repentant and sorry for what you've done. I don't believe it for a second." He gave me a cold look. "No, no, I don't. You say you are sorry for bringing people into the country to pray, but I know you aren't. I know that if you had not been caught, you'd still be bringing groups in. You are just sorry you got caught."

I sat as still as I could and tried not to react.

"You know why I know this? It's because you aren't just a Christian. You are a pastor. You are a missionary. You are hard-core."

"I admitted I am a pastor and a missionary," I said in a low-key, very calm, nonthreatening voice.

"Of course you have, and I know what that means. You are just trying to get out of this mess you got yourself into. 'I'm sorry,' you say, hoping we will let you go, but you aren't sorry at all. You just said what you had to say so that maybe we would go easy on you and send you back where you came from." He paused and then said with a sinister-sounding voice, "Didn't you?"

"I am a man of my word," I said.

"Your word? Ha. Why should I believe anything you say?" Prosecutor Min said. He pointed down at the stack of papers in front of him. "You admitted to trying to overthrow our government and to spreading lies about our Great Leader. You signed this confession. You yourself said you are guilty of everything."

His voice did not rise in anger as Mr. Park's had done. Instead, he had a very cold, calculating quality about him.

"You confessed you are a liar. And now you are telling the truth when you say you are sorry? No, you are not sorry, and I'm going to make sure you get what you deserve for what you have done. We're going to make an example of you so that no other 'missionary' dares come into our great nation and tries what you did."

"Okay," I said. I did not react. I had heard threats many times before. I was starting to get used to it.

"Now as for you and your case: Where were you born?" he asked. This was followed by more of the same questions I had answered a thousand times in Rason. "When did you move to the United States? . . . Tell me about your father . . ."

Min's line of questioning sounded like he had decided to start the whole process over from the beginning. I did not understand why. He came back the next day and went through the same routine, and then the next day and the next and the next. Every morning I expected Mr. Lee to walk through my door, but it was always Mr. Min who came in to question me.

I started worrying about what might have happened to Mr. Lee. I was afraid he had gotten into trouble for treating me too well. Giving a dangerous criminal candy and soda can land you into a lot of trouble in this place.

For weeks Prosecutor Min came to question me every day. Each session followed the same pattern. He asked me more questions I had already answered, and then he threatened me. "You are the worst American criminal since the Korean War. You not only tried to overthrow the government but you have mobilized, trained, and sent people here to participate in such an act," he told me. "I am going to make sure you get what's coming to you."

The daily grind of his berating took its toll. Not only did I have to listen to Prosecutor Min rail against me, my nights were filled with hours of anti-American propaganda on North Korean television. I felt a spirit of warfare all around me.

Late one night the warfare became very personal. I was sleeping when I felt hands around my throat, choking me. I struggled to breathe. I tried to reach up and pull the hands off of my throat, but my hands refused to move. My entire body felt pinned to the bed, as if someone were sitting on top of me. The weight grew heavier and heavier. I gasped for breath.

Finally, I managed to open my eyes. No one was on me. No hands were around my neck, yet the choking continued, and the weight grew heavier.

"*Jesus!*" I yelled.

Whatever had me let go.

"In the name of Jesus, get out! You filthy, evil spirit, get out!"

The oppression and warfare I had felt in my room evaporated as the peace of God filled the place. I went back to sleep and slept like a baby.

During the pretrial period I decided to put some order into my day. I wanted to have a schedule: three hours of worship, three hours of prayer, three hours of Bible reading, and three hours of exercise.

Whenever the prosecutor was not in my room, I sang praise songs to God in both English and Korean. Then I spent time praying. I didn't have anyone else to talk to, so three hours of talking to God went by really fast. Then I spent time reading my Bible. Finally, I spent three hours a day exercising. The guards didn't like it, but the chief prosecutor gave me permission to walk around my room.

My room was five meters wide, so one trip back and forth equaled ten meters. I started off doing one hundred laps a day, or one kilometer (about six-tenths of a mile). Eventually I increased this to two hundred laps, then three hundred and five hundred, until I eventually got up to one thousand laps, or ten kilometers, which is around six miles. I also did some push-ups and other calisthenics.

I did not get to follow this routine every day, but I tried. Having order and a schedule to my day helped me cope with the pressures I faced. However, the intensity of the pressure grew until I didn't think I could hold up any longer. But then God showed up again in a very surprising way.

One morning during my worship time, I started to crave a certain cold noodle soup for which one of the Pyongyang restaurants is famous. I'd had it on an earlier trip to Pyongyang. For some reason I could not stop thinking about this soup. I could almost smell it and taste it. However, I didn't dare ask the guards or one of the prosecutors to bring it to me, not with all the talk of war flying around. I didn't even pray for something so small. Instead, I just said to myself, *I really wish I had some of that cold noodle soup.*

The next day, when lunch arrived, I discovered a bowl of the exact cold noodle soup I had craved. The guard told me that they had someone bring it from the very restaurant I had in mind.

I could not believe my eyes. The soup was the first meal I truly enjoyed since my arrest. I savored every drop.

A day or so later I had a strong craving for some kimchi fried rice. Again, I did not dare ask for it, nor did I let anyone know I craved it. I didn't even pray for it.

That night when they brought in my dinner, I found the kimchi fried rice I had craved in the morning. It was almost as if I had phoned room service and placed my order directly.

The next day I craved tofu soup. When it came in my next meal, I realized it was more than a coincidence. Psalm 37:4 says, "Take delight in the LORD, and he will give you the desires of your heart." God was doing exactly that for me.

Over the course of my five months in the Pyongyang detention center, I counted at least forty times when God gave me the exact food I craved. By providing the food I desired, he let me know that he had not forgotten me. God not only gave me the desires of my heart but also of my stomach! He was with me, and he was not going to let anything happen to me that didn't go through him first.

Prosecutor Min walked into my room one morning in February 2013 and started in on me as he always did. "You are going to go to trial, and you are going to get the maximum penalty!" he said. He waved my confession at me. "You are going to get what you deserve. I will see to it."

Finally I could not take it any longer. "You know what? I'm done. I'm not going along with this anymore," I said.

"You what?" Min asked, shocked.

"The confession, the questions, all of it. I am done."

"What do you mean you are done? You signed this. You cannot take it back." Min was indignant.

"I signed it only because I was promised I would go home if I did. I didn't come into your country to try to overthrow the government. I brought people in to pray. All I ever wanted to do was help the North Korean people and let them know God loves them. The North Korean people with whom I worked will tell you that I always operated my business with integrity and respect for your country and culture. This whole mess started because I accidentally brought in an external computer hard drive that would never have been taken out of my briefcase until I got back to my home, except your people pulled it out and made a big deal about it. I apologized for bringing it in. I was not going to share anything on it with anyone in this country. So that's what I mean by I am done. I am not going along with this anymore."

"Are you accusing our people of forcing you to sign false documents?" Min said, seething.

"I'm not accusing anyone of anything. I'm just telling you what happened. And what happened was I was told that if I signed those papers and went along with everything, I was going to get to go home," I said.

"You are going to get what you deserve, and I will see to it," he growled. With that he stormed out of the room.

I let out a long sigh of relief. I guess I should have been worried about what might happen next, but to be honest, I didn't see how things could get much worse than they already were. Whether I went along with their charade or not, I still faced a trial for crimes that carried a death sentence. Cooperating had not made things any easier for me, not that I could see. I might as well try a new approach.

The chief prosecutor came to see me the next day, along with two other official-looking men in suits. The two new guys did not introduce themselves to me.

"What is this I hear about you changing your mind?" the chief prosecutor said, his voice rising. Clearly I had made him angry. "Now you are denying everything, are you? You say you don't have to do this anymore. Well, neither do we. We can just end it all right here and now if we want."

He did not explain what he meant by that, but I had a pretty good idea.

"You know," he continued, "I may just move you to a prison right now, today. We are pretty much done with this whole pretrial process." He stopped for a moment as if he were thinking about what he was going to say next. "I don't think I will do that, not until we decide what we need to do with you permanently. But I do think we need to make some changes. I think you must be too comfortable here. That's why you say the things you do. You think you can just take advantage of our kindness. So I've decided you will receive no more letters from your family."

Since my initial stack of letters I had received more mail every couple of weeks.

"You say you don't want to cooperate. Fine. But I have the power to make you suffer, and you are going to suffer." He then spun around on his heels and left, the two men in suits with him.

The next morning Mr. Lee returned for the first time in weeks. I was very glad to see him. "Where have you been?" I asked.

"I had to attend some other business in another city. It seems things went poorly while I was away. Come, let's go for a walk and have a little talk."

Mr. Lee led me out of the building and into an adjacent courtyard. I didn't think he just wanted to give me a little fresh air and sunshine. My room, like the one in Rason, had cameras. Mr. Lee needed to get me to a place where we could have a private conversation.

"So what happened?" he asked. "Why did you say you are no longer going to cooperate?"

"I thought you were gone, and the new prosecutor kept telling me I was going to go to trial and get what was coming to me. And that means I am going to have to serve whatever sentence they give me. I thought that if I was going to go down anyway, I might as well take a stand."

"No, no, no," Mr. Lee said. "You do not understand the seriousness of the situation in which you find yourself. These people are very angry. The whole country is. They are serious when they say they may apply a real-time resolution to you, which means taking you out into the square and shooting you as a war criminal. The war with America is about to start. They are angry. If you keep this up, you will die."

By this point I had heard so many threats against my life that I had a hard time taking them seriously. But Mr. Lee did. He truly believed my life was in danger.

"The best thing you can do is to cooperate and go along with everything to the end. You are not the first American we have held here. Every one of our previous prisoners eventually went home. You will, too, but not if you choose the route you announced to Mr. Min. If you stick with that, there's no turning back."

I thought about what he was saying as we walked back and forth through the courtyard. "Okay," I said, "I will cooperate. I will not take back my confession. I'll do whatever it takes to just end this and get me home."

Mr. Lee looked very relieved. He let out a small sigh. "You have made the right choice, Mr. Bae." I hoped he was right.

I returned to my room, sat down in my chair, and reflected on all that had just happened. I did not know who or what to believe. I did not know if the anger and threats were just part of a show to scare me, or if Mr. Min and the chief prosecutor meant business. The very idea that all these officials and the entire country believed war with the United States was imminent was hard for me to believe. *But if they truly believe it, anything might happen to me*, I thought.

As I sat there, reflecting on the uncertainty surrounding me, Graham Kendrick's song "Knowing You" started playing in my head, as if someone had just turned on a radio. Before I knew it I found myself singing, softly at first, then louder and louder.

I kept singing "Knowing You" over and over and over. I did not know if I would ever see my family again or even if I was going to get out of North Korea alive, but one thing I did know: I was not alone. My Savior was with me. He was all I had. And right now, he was enough.

————————————————————————

TWELVE

GUILTY AS CHARGED

> *The LORD will keep you from all harm—*
>   *he will watch over your life;*
> *the LORD will watch over your coming and going*
>   *both now and forevermore.*
>
> —PSALM 121:7–8

IN SPITE OF all the talk of my imminent trial, I still held out hope that one day Mr. Lee or the chief prosecutor might walk into my room and tell me I was going home right away. I kept marking off the days on my countdown calendars. I'd gone through several thirty-day countdowns so far. Mr. Lee did come in one day in late March to talk about my trial, but instead of letting me go home, he made it clear why the DPRK was so intent on me answering for my crimes.

"You must go on trial if anyone is going to take our laws seriously," he explained. "If we do not try you, we will encourage more missionaries to come into our country, thinking that if they get caught, the worst that will happen is they will be sent home. It has already been decided that we will make an example of you."

I didn't like the sound of that. He told me in February that I was to stand trial in March. Yet with March winding down without a trial, I entertained thoughts that perhaps I had been made example enough.

The chief prosecutor put those thoughts to rest. "There was no trial in March because of the current situation with the United States," he said. Apparently everyone was so preoccupied with preparing for war with America that they didn't have time to mess with a nobody like me.

The delay in the trial worked out well for me. The prosecutors rarely came around anymore, which gave me more time for worship, prayer, Bible reading, and exercise. Pyongyang television started broadcasting two hours earlier, which meant I had to cut everything off at three o'clock to spend the next seven and a half hours in front of the television. Supreme Leader Kim Jong Un's face was all over every channel for much of the time. I was never so thankful for anything as I was for the power outages that cut off the television so that I didn't have to look at him.

I caught a break from time to time thanks to the Science and Technology Channel, which broadcast only at night. It sometimes featured foreign education programs and even foreign films. One day I could not believe my eyes or ears: the channel showed *Finding Nemo* in English. Apparently they put it on the air to help students improve their English skills. I didn't care why they showed it. After sitting in the room all by myself, watching nothing but propaganda for seven hours every single day, to see an actual American animation in English was like finding a cool stream in the desert. I wept all the way through *Finding Nemo*. It was something from home, a taste of America.

In late March the chief prosecutor finally allowed me to receive mail from my family again. I went to meet the Swedish ambassador at the Yanggakdo Hotel again, and he brought a large stack of mail along with some packages.

I read my wife's letters first. My heart could hardly take it. She wrote:

> This winter we have had to walk in the dark tunnel where we could
> see no end. It has been so difficult for us, and it still has not ended yet.

However, we are walking together in this unbearable journey. As you know, the sunshine is hiding behind the cloud and the rainbow will be appearing after the storm . . . I desperately await good news from you, under the North Korean sky. Remember your family is waiting for you, full of love and cheer.

I reread over and over the line, "We are walking together in this unbearable journey." Her words made me feel as if she were right there with me. Knowing we were walking this journey together gave me strength not to give up.

Lydia also mentioned that she had shut down my ministry, closed my office, and removed all my furniture. Reading that was also hard for me. I'd been in custody for nearly six months with no end in sight. Closing my office was the right thing to do, and I knew I could reopen it when I resumed my work, but that seemed very far off now. I started to wonder if my work in China was ever going to continue, much less my work in North Korea.

Tucked into the stack of letters from my family was one from someone whose name I did not recognize. I opened it only to find it was not just one letter but several short notes from students at a church that had financially supported my missionary work. A group from the church had even joined me on one of my earlier Rason tours. I don't know how they learned I was in prison or even how they knew where to send the letters to get them to me. Not that it mattered.

Reading their short, encouraging notes recharged my spirit. "You are not forgotten but the eyes of the Lord are fixed upon you," one read. Another said, "God always has a plan, and even though right now it's a struggle, you'll definitely pull through." One wrote just to thank me for my faithfulness, while several more reminded me that God loves me and so did they.

Now I knew I really wasn't in this alone. God was already working in other people's lives through my imprisonment. I was excited to see what he was going to do next.

In late April the chief prosecutor came back to see me. "You will stand trial on April 30," he said, "so you need to prepare yourself."

I didn't know what I was supposed to prepare. I knew the outcome of the trial was already determined.

He continued, "You have the option of having a defense attorney for the trial, if you would like one. Think about it and let me know what you want to do."

I didn't know what I was supposed to think over, because the prosecutor's offer struck me as absurd. What good was a defense lawyer going to do me in North Korea, since they all work for the government anyway? The prosecutors and defenders are all on the same side. I understood the chief prosecutor's real motive. If I accepted, he could say, "Yes, we gave Mr. Bae a fair trial. He even had an attorney present to represent him." If I declined, he could say I had only myself to blame for the trial's outcome.

After much thought, I decided, why not? I had nothing to lose by having a "defense" lawyer at my side. And maybe the offer was sincere. I doubted it was, but I decided to give them the benefit of the doubt, just in case.

When the chief prosecutor came back the next day, he asked me what I thought of his offer.

"Can I at least meet my lawyer before I make up my mind?" I asked.

The chief prosecutor reacted as if this were the most absurd idea he'd ever heard. "No. That's not possible," he said.

"Then when am I going to see my lawyer?" I asked. I expected to have some time with him to prepare my defense.

"At the trial," the prosecutor said, as though the answer were obvious.

"Then I decline the offer and will defend myself," I said.

My defense was going to be pretty simple. I planned on admitting to everything. I was going to plead guilty and then ask for mercy. What else could I do?

"As you wish," the chief prosecutor said. Then he added, "Do you want the trial to be public or private?"

"What is the difference?"

"If it is public we will broadcast it so the media from around the world can pick it up. Private means no one will see it except for the people in the courtroom," the prosecutor explained.

For me, the choice was easy. I did not want publicity, but not because I was shy. Even now, as I faced the prospect of being tried and convicted of crimes carrying a possible death penalty, I thought it best to keep the entire business as low-key as possible so as not to embarrass the North Korean government. I still held out hope that once everything was resolved I might be able to return to my work in the country.

"Private," I replied. "However, I would like for the Swedish ambassador to be there." The Swedish ambassador remained my only contact with the outside world. I thought that perhaps his presence might give the North Korean authorities second thoughts about putting on a show trial. With him there, I might have a better chance at justice.

"No," the chief prosecutor said. "You may have the Swedish delegation there only if the trial is public. Then all the press will come too. Private means private. No one from the outside."

"Never mind then," I said.

Even after this discussion, I still found it hard to believe that I was actually going to be tried for crimes against North Korea. I was far from the first foreigner arrested for illegal activity in the DPRK. Almost all had been released after a few months without the formality of a trial. The most notable exception had been Laura Ling and Euna Lee, who were arrested when they, along with a film crew, walked across a frozen Tumen River from China into North Korea. They received a sentence of twelve years of hard labor for committing hostile acts against the DPRK government. But shortly after the trial was over, Laura and Euna were released because Bill Clinton flew over to negotiate for them. Their detention lasted only four and a half months.

The fact that they were released so quickly made me think that my trial was not necessary. I had already confessed, and I had been in custody for six months. What more could they want from me?

The next time Prosecutor Lee came to see me, I asked him these questions.

"You must stand trial to make it clear to the world that you have not been imprisoned unjustly. It is necessary to show that you are the aggressor and we are the victim," he said.

"I'm not sure that I follow you," I said.

"It is simple. You came into our great nation and committed hostile acts. You say it was just prayer, but prayer is a hostile act because it calls into question everything our system is based upon. Then you trained North Koreans to do mission work for you. That, too, is a hostile act. Even your worship and your Bible—both are hostile when you see them in the context of our laws and our juche system. Already there have been calls for your release from United States officials and the Western media. They say you are innocent and have been arrested unjustly. The trial will show the world you are not innocent, that you have done exactly what we have accused you of doing." His words did not come out as mean or threatening. Mr. Lee simply explained the situation exactly as he understood it.

I guess I looked a little downcast after he said these things, because he added, "Don't worry about the outcome of the trial or the sentence you are given. The number of years you hear are not important. It does not matter what happens during the trial. The important thing is what comes after the trial and how your government responds to it. It is like when your child breaks a neighbor's window. You as the parent must go make things right for your child. First, you apologize for what your child has done; then you compensate your neighbor for his broken window. That is what we expect from the United States government. We need them to understand what you have done so that they will come and apologize for their child and make things right."

For the first time it occurred to me that my case was not really about me. *I'm a bargaining chip, a way for North Korea to make America look bad.*

Relations between the two countries, at least on the North Korean side, continued to deteriorate. Talk of war dominated the nightly news. Video footage showed Kim Jong Un conducting a war strategy meeting. He pointed at different places on the US map spread out before him to make it look like he was saying, "We will drop bombs here and here and here."

Yet the North Koreans did not see themselves as the aggressors. In conversations with Mr. Lee and other officials, it was clear that these people truly believed they were victims of America's bullying. "We are a small country," they said. "Why is this big country pushing us around?"

The DPRK government has a policy of "military first." That is, their first spending priority is to build up the military to protect themselves against the inevitable United States attack. "That's why we suffer with shortages," I was told. "We have to spend so much to protect ourselves from you that very little is left over. If America would just leave us alone, we would not suffer like we do. We would have more food, happier lives, and peace."

Once I made this connection, I started to see my place in the larger context of the relations between the two countries. In the eyes of the North Korean people, when Clinton negotiated for Ling and Lee's release, he also came to apologize, like the parent whose child broke the window. The people saw this as a sign that they were winning against America, that the United States was bowing down to them.

That was the endgame for me. They wanted a former president to once again humble himself before the Supreme Leader and plead for mercy for one of America's naughty children. That is why I had to go on trial and answer for my crimes. In North Korea's eyes, all of America was really on trial with me. I would not fully understand all the implications of this until much later.

One week before the scheduled start of my trial, the chief prosecutor had me phone my family. I don't think he meant it as a humanitarian gesture.

"Tell your family to contact your government and tell the president to request special amnesty for you. That's the only way you will get to go home," he instructed me.

I relayed his message word for word first to my wife and then to my sister and my mother. All of them became upset over hearing that I was actually going to stand trial, but I calmed them as best I could.

"Other people have had to go to court," I told them. "I have to go through the trial before any resolution can happen between the United States and North Korea. So, whatever sentence I might receive, do not worry about it too much. I am sure everything will be resolved soon."

When I explained this to my sister, Terri, she said, "Okay," but I don't think she was convinced. Terri had already written Secretary of State John Kerry and asked him to do everything in his power to bring me home. Up to this point she had also honored my request and had not gone to the media to appeal for my release. I still believed the United States and North Korean governments wanted to work out my release quietly. But it was hard for Terri to sit back and do nothing and let the process play out.

I was allowed to see the Swedish ambassador, Mr. Andersson, and his assistant, Mr. Svensson, the day I called my family. We met at the same hotel where we had met the first time. Mr. Andersson was eager to discuss my upcoming trial.

"Are you going to have an attorney represent you?" he wanted to know.

"I decided against it," I said.

"No, you must have an attorney with you," he said. He sounded very concerned. "We will make sure that you have one." I thanked him. He also said that they would attend the trial even though his North Korean counterpart had insisted that was impossible.

Whether the Swedes were there or not probably didn't matter. I knew that the outcome of the trial had already been decided. The only question was how long of a sentence the court would give me.

I also knew that if I had been a North Korean citizen, there would be no question. I would already be dead.

My trial lasted an hour and a half, including the time it took the judge to decide my fate. I stood in a witness stand throughout the proceedings, rather than sitting behind a desk as one would in an American court-room. I wore a suit I had asked my wife to send me for the occasion. Based on the little I knew about trials from watching movies and tele-vision, I thought I needed to look my best.

My plan didn't exactly work. When I put on the suit, I looked like a boy wearing his father's clothes. I did not realize that I already had lost at least thirty pounds.

No lawyer came in to represent me. Apparently the Swedes were unable to get one for me. My judge sat in the front of the courtroom, with two judges sitting next to him, one on either side. The extra judges were there to ensure everything was conducted according to the rule of law. A court reporter sat at a desk and typed out everything that was said. Mr. Lee and Mr. Min sat in the audience, while the chief prosecu-tor stood on the side of the room opposite me.

The trial began with the chief prosecutor reading the charges against me: "We hereby charge the American criminal, Bae Junho, with crimes against the state. Specifically, we charge him with the following:

"Working with the evangelical organization Youth With A Mission (YWAM) and preaching against the North Korean government in American and South Korean churches.

"Planning an anti–North Korean religious coup d'état called 'Operation Jericho,' so named for a biblical city which was destroyed by the Israelite army. His coup began in the United States, South Korea, and China long before Bae traveled to North Korea.

"Setting up bases in China for the purpose of toppling the Democratic People's Republic of Korea. He then brought people into the country to pray while disguising them as tourists.

"Encouraging North Korean citizens to bring down the government.

"Conducting a malignant smear campaign against the government of North Korea and our Supreme Leader."

The YWAM reference was significant because YWAM's founder, Loren Cunningham, had been on the DPRK's radar for some time. In 2006 Cunningham delivered a sermon in which he urged the printing of seven million Korean Bibles, one for every family in North Korea, in preparation for the day when North Korea's borders open. To the DPRK, this was like a declaration of war. The Bible is viewed as a dangerous weapon. They even have one on display in an anti-American propaganda museum filled with weapons the United States used against them during the Korean War.

After reading the charges against me, the chief prosecutor then called his one and only witness, Songyi, the North Korean woman who went through our discipleship training program before returning to North Korea to start a Christian orphanage. She appeared very nervous as she took her place in the witness stand. I tried to convey compassion in the way I looked at her, but I am not sure she noticed. Songyi did her best to avoid looking my way.

"Do you know this man, Bae Junho?" the prosecutor asked.

"Yes," she replied.

"Did you receive biblical training from this man while you were in China?"

"Yes."

"Did he tell you to return to North Korea?"

"Yes."

"Did he give you an assignment to fulfill once you returned?"

"Yes. He told me to start an orphanage for the street children and raise them in the Christian way."

"No further questions," the prosecutor said.

The judge then turned to me. "Do you have any questions for the witness?" he asked me.

"No, sir," I said.

The judge then dismissed Songyi, who quickly left the courtroom.

After the trial I asked Mr. Lee about her. He told me he dropped her off at her home and that she was going to be fine. "Since she told the truth, she will be taken care of," he told me. I wasn't so sure, but I went back to the promise God had made me on my third day of detainment. He had promised no one would be harmed. I claimed this promise for Songyi.

After Songyi's testimony the chief prosecutor read a signed statement from Sam, my friend who operated the coffee shop in the hotel where I was arrested. In his statement he told how I wanted to start a prayer center in Rason. He also described the orientation talk in which I spoke of the seven spirits that ruled North Korea.

The prosecutor then turned to video evidence against me. They flashed on the video screen a photo of one of the symbols my staff created for my ministry. Using Photoshop, a staff member had created the word *Hope* out of a North Korean flag with ragged edges. To the DPRK, desecrating their flag was the ultimate insult.

"See," he said to me, "this is the kind of hope you want to bring to our people by bringing down our government."

They also showed brief clips of some of the videos they found on my hard drive. Images of starving children on the streets of North Korea came up on the screen. The fact that I had not created this video, nor did I even know it was on my hard drive, did not matter.

"You see, your honor," the prosecutor said to the judge, "the evidence is overwhelming. This man is guilty. He has violated Article 60 of our constitution." The judge appeared to agree.

"However, Bae Junho has shown remorse and has apologized," the prosecutor added. "Therefore I ask that we show him mercy by giving him only fifteen years of hard labor."

This was the first time I had heard fifteen years mentioned, although Mr. Lee had hinted that they were going to seek a lighter sentence. Fifteen years did not seem like a light sentence, but I guess it was in comparison to a death sentence.

After the prosecutor concluded the case against me, the judge asked me, "Do you have anything to say to the court before we consider the evidence against you?"

I had given this moment a great deal of thought since it had first become clear to me that I was going to go on trial. Mr. Lee had even asked me to write out what I was going to say and give it to him ahead of time. Clearly, I could not protest my innocence, not after signing a confession. However, I wanted to explain why I did what I did and to make it clear that I truly love the North Korean people.

I began, "Honorable Judge, first I want to acknowledge my wrongdoings against the government of the Democratic People's Republic of Korea and its leadership. During the six months I have spent in the DPRK, I have come to understand that my actions have severely violated your constitution. I realize that my teachings against the DPRK leadership have damaged the reputation and creditability of the government.

"Second, therefore, I want to apologize for my actions against the government of the DPRK and its leadership. I deeply regret my actions, and I want to sincerely apologize for all my wrongdoings and my actions that have offended so many.

"Third, I am ready to accept the consequences for my actions. I have learned that I have violated Article 60 of your constitution and my actions are not tolerable according to your laws. I fully accept whatever penalty my actions may bring.

"Lastly, although I am ready to accept my consequences, I would like to ask you to give me a chance to become a bridge that connects the West and the DPRK. There are more than twelve million Christians in South Korea and more than fifty thousand churches. There are another ten million Buddhists in South Korea as well. As a Korean, I want to see the two Koreas unified someday. When the countries are unified, how are you going to get along with people of faith? In a unified Korea, we need to learn to acknowledge our differences, accept one another, and live together harmoniously. Even President Kim Il Sung once said that, as long as people are for the unification of Korea and for the people of

Korea, he is willing to work with anyone, regardless of their faith, background, and origin.

"I am a Christian, and I have tried to live by the Christian doctrines throughout my life. I am here in this court because of my belief in God. As I already have acknowledged, apologized, and accepted the consequences of my actions, I am asking you to give me another chance to become a bridge for the unification and the prosperity of the people of this land, even though my wrongdoings are punishable by a heavy sentence. What good would it do to send me to a labor camp? I am asking for your mercy today."

After I finished, the judge said, "I will now go and consider my decision."

Fifteen minutes later he returned. In a decision that surprised no one, he said, "I find the defendant guilty and sentence him to fifteen years hard labor. Court is dismissed."

Prosecutor Lee responded to the fifteen-year sentence as though I had just been acquitted. Later I learned that before the trial he had worked hard for a lighter sentence for me. The other prosecutors really had planned on trying me as a war criminal and sentencing me to life in prison. But Mr. Lee pushed for leniency. By the time my trial started, tensions with the United States had cooled somewhat, which helped the other prosecutors go along with Mr. Lee.

Later in the summer, the chief prosecutor said to me, "You owe your life to that man."

I had to agree.

THIRTEEN

103

Now I want you to know, brothers and sisters, that what has happened to me has actually served to advance the gospel. As a result, it has become clear throughout the whole palace guard and to everyone else that I am in chains for Christ.

—PHILIPPIANS 1:12–13

A FEW DAYS after my conviction, I was taken to a local hospital for a full medical evaluation. I'd had a similar examination right after my arrest to determine whether I was strong enough to withstand the rigors of the weeks of interrogation before me. I had thought the earlier examination was primarily designed to rattle me and make me believe I would be tortured if I did not talk. All of that was now behind me. This examination would determine if I was physically fit enough to spend the next fifteen years working on a prison farm in a labor camp.

I believed the answer was a foregone conclusion. With my long list of medical conditions, I did not believe there was any way a doctor would deem me fit for a hard labor camp. Mr. Lee even told me as much in a conversation right after my conviction.

A day or two after my medical examination, and before I got the results back, I was allowed to call my family. However, the chief prosecutor wrote out a script I had to follow in the calls to my wife, mother, and sister.

"You must tell them to contact your government and tell them to make the most ardent efforts for the following: the United States needs to validate the DPRK legal system; they must acknowledge your guilt; they must apologize for your crimes; and they must promise that these types of illegal acts by Americans will not happen again," he told me.

I had so much I wanted to say to my family that I didn't get to. Once I recited the lines the chief prosecutor gave me, he told me to hang up and make the next call. However, I was able to reassure my wife, mother, and sister that although I faced a fifteen-year sentence, I didn't think I was going to be sent to a camp.

"Their doctors have examined me, so my chances of going to the camp are small. Don't worry," I said. "Everything will work out. I will be fine."

The next day the Swedish ambassador came to see me. I gave him a list of my medical conditions, and he seemed very concerned. The embassy then made a formal request of the DPRK government that my conditions be treated before my sentence was carried out.

We all thought that there was no way any doctor would clear me to go to the camp, but I was still nervous when Mr. Lee and the chief prosecutor took me back to the hospital for a meeting with the hospital director and the primary doctor who had examined me. The five of us sat down in a hospital conference room. The chief prosecutor seemed anxious to get on with the proceedings, so there were no introductions. He opened with, "So what did you decide?"

The hospital director, a woman in her fifties, took the question. "Based on the results of our tests, we have determined that the patient, Mr. Bae, is not fit to work in the labor camp."

I wanted to give her a huge hug. I felt as though she had just saved my life.

"Can he at least do some light labor in the camp without doing everything other inmates might be asked to do?" the chief prosecutor asked.

I held my breath. I did not know the difference between light labor and hard labor in the North Korean system. The answer to this question was going to determine whether I was on my way to the prison.

"No," the director said. "He needs regular exercise for his diabetes, but his overall condition, including his injured back, makes him ill fitted for even light labor."

I looked the director in the eyes and gave her a look that I hoped expressed my extreme gratitude. I dared not say a word. In this system one never knows what might be perceived as insubordination. Instead I sat, took in her words, and thanked her in my heart. Outwardly I showed no emotion.

The chief prosecutor did not want to give up. "Are you sure?" he asked.

"Yes, we are sure," the director said. "This man is not fit for the labor camp, not now at least."

With that, the meeting ended. I was taken back across town to the detention center. Mr. Lee came to see me in my room. As soon as he walked in, he said in an agitated voice, "Why didn't you speak up and tell the chief prosecutor that you are too weak to go to the labor camp?"

His question surprised me. "I didn't think I needed to say anything, because the director was saying that for me. What am I going to add that is going to carry more weight than the director?"

"You should have said something," Mr. Lee insisted. "You need to complain a little more and make it clear that you cannot stand up to the rigors of the labor camp."

"Do you think that would matter?" I asked.

"Very much," Mr. Lee said.

I did not understand Mr. Lee's logic until three days later, when the chief prosecutor walked into my room and shouted, "Gather your things. You are going to the labor camp today to begin serving out your sentence."

"What?" I asked.

The chief prosecutor was very upset. Steam came out of his ears. "Your Western media is mocking our judicial system. They think it is a joke and reported it was an unjust trial because it lasted only an hour and a half. We went through four and a half months of pretrial procedures. They think you are an innocent man who is being held as a political bargaining chip! No. You are clearly guilty and deserve to go to the labor camp! So that's where you are going. *Now!*"

I had not anticipated hearing these words. The North Korean government was clearly upset about the way the Western media reported the results of my trial. Now they had decided to raise the stakes by actually sending me to the labor camp in spite of the doctor's recommendation.

I realized the North Korean government wanted to see how far they could push the US government. Because I was caught in the middle of a high-stakes game of chicken, I was about to become the first American sent to a labor camp since the Korean War.

The prosecutor spun around and walked out of the room. A guard came in as soon as he left and said, "Sit down in the chair."

I started to argue that I had just been told to gather my things, but I thought better of it. Another guard brought a barber to my room. "Sit down," I was told again.

I sat. The barber put a sheet around me, pulled out his clippers, and shaved my head. I felt as if I were in an old army movie.

The chief prosecutor returned a few minutes later to take me out of what had been my home for nearly six months. "Don't you think you should say a good-bye prayer over this place before you go?" he said in a mocking tone.

"I've prayed enough here already," I replied. I felt certain he was thinking, *And look where all that prayer got you—fifteen years in a labor camp!*

With that, the prosecutor and guards escorted me out of the Pyongyang detention center for the last time and placed me in a minivan with black curtains covering the windows. Once again I was stuck in the middle of the backseat, only this time I was handcuffed. I had never been handcuffed before.

To be honest, I was a little excited about going to the prison. I did not want to be in prison, obviously, but after being isolated for the past six months, I looked forward to interacting with the other inmates.

I thought back to a conversation I had had with one of the guys in my tour group during our train ride from Dandong to Yanji six months earlier. Like I always did, I had gone over all the things they should not do in North Korea. The guy had joked, "I guess if something happens, we can start a prison ministry." I had laughed.

Riding to the prison, my head down between my knees so I could not see where I was being taken, I remembered the conversation. *That's exactly what I am going to do*, I told myself. If I was going to have to spend time in a labor camp, I was going to do what I had come to North Korea to do. I was going to be a missionary. *Inmates will probably be more receptive to what I have to say than the guards and prosecutors back in Rason and Pyongyang were*, I thought.

About twenty-five minutes after we had left the detention center, our van came to a stop. "Get out. We're here," a guard said.

It took my eyes a moment to adjust once I was out of the van. I expected to see the kind of prison I had seen in the movies, something with large walls and guard towers and inmates milling about the yard. Instead, I found myself inside a fence, with a single-story building off to one side and a taller building, perhaps four or five stories tall, next to it. The single-story building was not large for a prison, perhaps five thousand square feet. To the side of the building was a large agricultural area that stretched up a hill. The fence around us was topped with razor wire and what looked to be an electric wire.

Both the chief prosecutor and Mr. Lee had come along for the ride. I expected them to get back in the van, but they walked beside me as one of the prison guards led me into the single-story building. Another man in a suit followed us with a video camera, taping everything that happened. When I happened to glance his way, he said, "Don't look at me!" He seemed to be in a very bad mood. Other officials and guards came in and out of the buildings, watching me. It seemed everyone had turned out to see the famous American criminal.

Once we were inside the building, I was escorted down the hall and into a small room. A large man in his fifties, who had to be at least two hundred pounds and was dressed in a suit and tie rather than a uniform, was in the room, along with guards and other officials. I had yet to see another inmate. No inmates were out in the prison yard. No inmates were working out in the fields. And I could not see any other inmates anywhere near this reception room.

The man in the suit told the guards, "I will take care of him from here." Because he told the other guards what to do, I at first thought he was the chief guard. But judging from his size and the way everyone jumped when he issued a command, I decided he must be the warden. No guard, even the chief guard, would be high enough in the party to be so heavy.

Turning to me, the man I believed was the warden said, "You need to change into your new uniform. Strip off your clothes."

"All my clothes?" I asked.

"Yes, everything. Even your underwear."

Once I was completely naked, a guard brought me a prison uniform. Over the left breast of the shirt was a patch with the number *103* stitched on it. The number became my new identity.

After I changed, I was handed a list with an inventory of all the items I had brought with me to the prison, including clothes, my Bibles, a handful of books my wife had sent me, and a few magazines the Swedish embassy had given me. I had to sign it. "All these things will be returned to you when you are released," I was told. I could not help but notice the list was already missing several personal items I had brought into North Korea back in November.

The man I assumed was the warden then started his welcome speech. "While you are here, you will answer to your inmate number, 103. No one is going to call you Junho or Mr. Bae or anything else. Your name is 103. And when one of the officers calls you 103, you are to respond, 'Yes, sir.' Do you understand, 103?"

"Yes, sir," I replied.

"We expect no trouble out of you while you are here. To make sure of that you must memorize the ten rules for this prison camp and the daily schedule you will follow." He pointed to two signs on the wall. "Memorize them now, 103."

The rules were simple enough. As best I can remember, they were:

1. You must obey the guards' commands and instructions perfectly at all times.
2. Do not call the guards by name. You must address the guards as *master* or *teacher.*
3. Do not talk back to the guards.
4. If you are sick, you have the right to see a doctor.
5. You must finish your work according to the assignment given. If you do not finish your work, you will be punished.
6. You may read books, including the Bible, newspapers, and magazines, and watch TV during assigned hours only.
7. You have the right to ask to see your country's consulate member. (This one told me I was in a special prison where only foreigners were held.)
8. You must clean your room and wash your clothes.
9. You must keep your hygiene clean and healthy at all times.
10. If you have any reasonable request, you can always ask the guard with respect.

"If you need something, 103, speak to me or one of the guards about it and we will do what we can," the warden said. "Your time with us does not have to be difficult. If you do what you are told and do not make any decisions on your own without first asking one of the officers, then you will be fine. How your time goes here is really up to you."

"Yes, sir. I understand," I replied. Causing trouble was the last thing on my mind. I was convinced I was going to be one of the only Christians the warden and guards and other officials in the prison would ever interact with. I was very aware that my behavior would either open doors to the gospel or close them, depending on how they viewed me.

There's an old saying: "You are the only Jesus some people will ever see." For me, this was actually the case.

After the warden's little welcome speech, the guards escorted me outside to the outer courtyard. One placed me next to a wall and said, "Stand still." Another official came over and snapped my official prison mug shot. I was then escorted down the hallway and to my cell. My new home was room 3—hence my new name, 103. However, I did not figure this out until right before I was released. I even asked one of the guards about my number. "Am I the 103rd inmate in this prison? Were there 102 people kept here before me?"

The guard told me to shut up. "It's not for you to know!" he told me in no uncertain terms.

Room 3 was about three hundred square feet and was made up of three small rooms. There was a living room area with a desk and a chair. On the opposite side was a television, which told me my reeducation was not yet complete. The room also had a window with bars across it. The window looked out to the interior hallway and on to the gate. There was also a bedroom with a twin bed, and a small bathroom. In addition to the camera hung in plain sight in the middle of the living room, more cameras hung on all the walls. Apparently, when it comes to prison accommodations in North Korea, this was as nice as it gets.

The prison doctor came into my room to check up on me. When I found out who he was, I said to him, "The doctor at the hospital said I was not fit enough to work here." I started to go through the list of my conditions when the doctor cut me off.

"Don't worry," the doctor said. "Everybody who comes here gets better. The work will make your symptoms go away. So will the healthy food you will eat here. You will be fine."

"I have medications for my diabetes and gallstones I need to take. My wife sent them to me," I said.

"I will take care of your medications," the doctor answered in a way that told me I didn't know what I was talking about.

"But—"

"Work is the best medicine. Your work will begin tomorrow," he said, ending the conversation.

The warden returned. "Again, 103, if you need something, just tell the guard. But make sure you do not harbor any illusions about escape. If you escape you will be shot." He motioned toward the guard standing just outside my door. "All the guards have real bullets in their guns, and they will use them on you."

"I understand," I said.

"I will let you settle into your room. You will start work first thing in the morning."

"What kind of work will I do?" I asked.

"You will work on the farm to help grow the food that we feed you. In juche, everyone must work and provide for their own needs. You will be no different."

Uh-oh, I thought. *If my eating depends on my agricultural skills, I am in serious trouble.*

The warden left, and lunch was brought in. It consisted of some simple noodles with a bit of pickle on top. In the evening they served me a dinner of some rice and two fish that were just a little bigger than anchovies. Mixed in with the rice I found two or three pieces of what I assumed was pork, but it was about 90 percent fat with just a tiny sliver of actual meat on one side. They also gave me a couple of vegetables and some broth. Breakfast the next day was more of the same. Compared to what I had eaten at the detention center, the meals were much simpler. I didn't know how long I could do hard labor with such meager meals.

Around ten o'clock on my first night, the guard finally gave me permission to go to bed. I lay down on my bed and pulled the thin blanket up over me. My overhead light was still on. I looked for a switch to turn it off but could not find one. I tried closing my eyes tight, but the light shone right through.

"Do you think it would be possible to turn the light off?" I asked the guard.

"No, 103, do not ask such a foolish thing. If the light is out, how will I be able to keep an eye on you?" the guard snapped back.

"Okay, thank you," I said. I didn't want to make the guards mad on my first day. Instead, I rolled over and tried to ignore the light. *Fifteen years of this*, I thought to myself. *Oh, Lord, please get me home.*

FOURTEEN ———————————————————

Down on the Farm

But he said to me, "My grace is sufficient for you, for my power is made perfect in weakness." Therefore I will boast all the more gladly about my weaknesses, so that Christ's power may rest on me. That is why, for Christ's sake, I delight in weaknesses, in insults, in hardships, in persecutions, in difficulties. For when I am weak, then I am strong.

—2 Corinthians 12:9–10

THE TALLEST KOREAN man I had ever met came into my room a little before eight o'clock on my first morning in the labor camp. He had to be at least six feet three inches tall.

"Good morning, 103. I am the acting deputy warden," he said. "I am the one who will make sure you complete the tasks assigned to you. Your work begins now. Follow me."

He led me out of my room, down the hall, and out into the field that ran up the side of a hill. I think the field covered about two acres. A stack of tools sat next to the field along with a bag that I assumed was filled with seeds. The tools included a wooden A-frame carrier that I wore on my back like a backpack. I used it to carry the bag of seed into the field. They also gave me a hoe. Thankfully, the deputy warden also gave me a ball cap to wear to keep some of the sun off of me. Three guards stood

137

near my equipment, all in full military uniform with sidearms, all with their arms crossed, all trying to look very, very tough.

"In this field you are going to plant and grow soybeans," the deputy warden announced. "We are self-reliant here in this camp. We grow what we eat and take care of ourselves just as we are taught in juche. You will learn this as well. It is a good system."

My only experience with soybeans before that moment had been eating tofu dishes. I had grown up in Seoul, a city of ten million people, and then moved to the Los Angeles area when I was sixteen. Before I walked out in that field, I had never even seen a soybean plant, much less tried to plant and grow one. For that matter, I had never planted *anything* before. I assumed—and hoped—it was as simple as digging a hole and dropping in the seed.

"This field is not large. You should be able to plant it in a few days at the most," he continued. "But you must go quickly. It is late in the season to just now be planting. If you are to harvest any beans, you need to get the seed in the ground now. Do you have any questions?"

"Where do you want me to start?" I asked.

"There," he said, pointing to a front corner of the field. "Work your way across in rows, one row at a time, moving up the hill. You will have a water break at ten o'clock, then lunch at twelve thirty, and another water break at three thirty. If you have completed all of your work, you will go back to your room at six. If you have not, you will stay in the field until your chore is finished. Now, go get started."

I walked over to my supplies. The three guards spread out in a triangle around me. One patted his sidearm to make sure I noticed it. I attached the seed bag to the A-frame and hoisted it onto my back. The weight of it dropping down pulled at the sore part of my back, making me wince. I said nothing and tried not to let on that anything bothered me.

I picked up the hoe and walked over to where I was supposed to start. The sun was not yet hot, but I could tell it was going to be a very warm day. I was already sweating, and I hadn't even started my work yet. I prayed I wasn't going to have to do this for the next fifteen years.

I set down my A-frame and bag of seeds and stared at the ground for a few moments, unsure of what to do first. The ground was hard and dry. A few weeds were sprinkled all along the hillside along with some grass. "Get the seed in the ground," I'd been told. Not knowing what else to do, I took the hoe and started digging. When I had a little hole a few inches deep, I reached into the bag, took out a seed, dropped down on my knees, and placed it in the hole. I then scooped the dirt back over the seed with my hands.

I stood up and noticed the guards staring at me. "What are you doing?" one of them asked.

"What do you mean, sir?" I replied. I had to call the guards *sir* even though all three were at least fifteen years younger than me. One looked to be about the same age as my son.

"You look like you've never done this before," he said.

"I haven't, sir," I said.

All three guards laughed. "Oh, come on. Seriously, 103, what are you doing? Why are you messing around like that?" another guard said.

"I'm not messing around, sir. I'm trying to plant these seeds."

"Have you ever done any farming before?" the first guard asked again.

"No, sir. Never," I said.

All three let out incredulous laughs. "Then how did you survive?" the third guard asked. "How can anybody live without knowing how to farm?"

"Where I come from, the farmers do all the farming, just like fishermen fish and carpenters build things," I said.

"How can a few farmers grow enough food for everybody?" one asked. He clearly did not believe me.

"The farms are very large. Farmers have tractors and plows and other machinery. With the right machines it doesn't take very many people to grow a lot of food," I replied.

The looks on the guards' faces made me feel as if I had just stepped into the Twilight Zone or as if I were some crazy person describing life on Mars.

"So what do you do to make a living?" the second guard asked.

"I talk, sir. I am a pastor and a missionary. I talk for a living."

The guards reacted as though this were the most absurd thing they had ever heard. "So you just talk with your mouth into a microphone or something? That's how you survive, huh?" the first guard said in a mocking tone.

"Yes, sir. That's right," I said. "I don't have to know how to farm or how to grow or catch my own food, because I can go to a supermarket filled with food I can buy."

I might as well have told them that birds fly into my house at night and deliver groceries to me. I think they might have found that story more believable. The three exchanged looks. Then the first guard said, "Enough talking. Get to work."

I dug another hole with the hoe and then stooped down to drop a seed in it. I repeated this a few times before the second guard, a young, thin guy, finally said, "Enough of this foolishness, 103. Let me show you how to do this right. If I don't, it will take you all summer to just get the field planted."

He grabbed my hoe and scraped out a little trench along the ground. "Like this, 103." The hoe looked like an extension of his arm, not a tool. He moved quickly and efficiently. "Now drop the seeds in the ground, spacing them out like this." He held out his hands about a foot from one another. "Then cover them over all at once. Do you think you can do that?"

"Yes, sir. I think so," I said. I reached into the bag and grabbed a handful of soybean seeds. I got back on my hands and knees and placed each seed exactly a foot apart. The guard shook his head. "Stand up to do it," he said.

I tried. The seeds never landed in the trench. I ended up on my knees anyway, picking the seeds up out of the weeds and placing them into the trench before scooping dirt back over them.

Over the next couple of hours, I tried to plant my seeds like the guard had shown me, but I wasn't very successful. My back and hands already hurt, and my day was just getting started. Thankfully, I had a short break at ten. The guards changed at eleven, with three new men watching over me. The new set of guards, dressed in full uniform, also spread out like a triangle around me, standing in the rising sun.

At twelve thirty I was told to eat. I took my lunch back in the room, out of the sun. Working all morning had made me very hungry, but the portions were no bigger than those of the day before. I had a few noodles, a little egg, and a couple of vegetables. My shirt was nearly soaked in sweat. I think I hurt more sitting still eating than I did working. At least when I was working, everything was moving. Once I sat down my muscles got tight, my back felt as if it were going to seize up, and my entire body felt as though it could just fall over.

I still had another four hours in the field to go.

I started back to work at one thirty, scraping away at the ground with my hoe. I noticed another field on the opposite side of a large fence. Out in the field I saw young men working, most stripped down to the waist. I recognized a couple of the men as the guards who had stood watch over me in the morning. Seeing them working on the farm only made sense. Everywhere I had been in North Korea, I had heard people preach their system of self-reliance. Everyone was supposed to find ways to provide for themselves. The other field looked to be the way the guards provided the food they needed in the prison.

I found the sight a little ironic. In the morning the men stood guard over me, forcing me to do the work that was my punishment for crimes against the state. In the afternoon they had to do the same work as I did, only theirs wasn't supposed to be punishment. Instead, planting beans in the heat of the afternoon was one of their rewards of juche. I wondered if they saw the irony.

As the afternoon grew hotter, my hoeing and planting grew slower. I could hardly straighten up after leaning over to dig with the hoe. My legs did not want to pick me back up after I dropped down to put the seeds in the dirt.

They expect me to do this for the next fifteen years? I thought. *I will not survive it. They know that.*

There's no way they will work me to death out here. They need me alive to do whatever it is they want to do to America.

I know my country is working to bring me home. Maybe I will get to go home in a month. I started a new thirty-day countdown in my head.

The guards changed shifts. The new crew spread out in another triangle around me, each one doing his best to look as menacing as possible. The sun was hot, and the air hardly moved. I noticed rivers of sweat running down the guards' faces.

These guys are as miserable as I am, I realized.

I didn't think I was such a dangerous criminal that three guards needed to watch over me. Maybe they had nothing else to do. As far as I could tell, I was the only prisoner in the entire labor camp.

To pass the time, I started singing praise songs. Most of the time I sang in English, although I threw in a few Korean songs as well. By late afternoon I didn't think I was going to survive to the end of the day. I started singing, "Swing low, sweet chariot, comin' for to carry me home . . ." I wished a chariot would come for to carry me home. I was ready to go.

After what felt like the longest day of my life, six o'clock came. I had not achieved all I was supposed to achieve for the day. I had planted only a few rows. Even though I had been warned I was going to have to stay out in the field until I finished that day's assignment, the deputy warden showed me some mercy. In all the months I worked out in the field, I think I had to work extra time only once or twice.

I went back to room 3. I just wanted to collapse on my bed. My dinner, which consisted of basically the same thing I'd had every meal so far, was waiting for me.

As soon as I finished eating, I headed toward my bedroom. The guard stopped me.

"Where are you going? It is not time for bed. Sit there." He pointed to the chair next to the desk. "The TV is to be on. You may also read if you like."

I was too tired to read, so I tried to focus on the television. The

Me with mom in 1971

Terri and me in 1975

My dad—the famous baseball manager—Terri, cousin Kirim as the catcher, and me in 1978

My family gathered around the piano

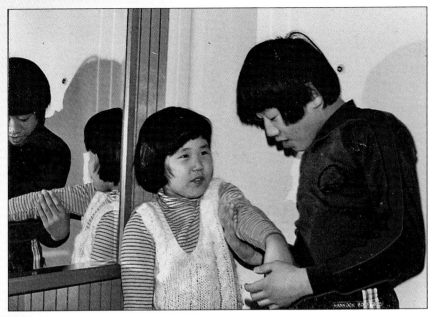

Me showing Terri how to swim in 1980

Me with Terri in 1987

Hanging out with college buddy
Bobby Lee, Eugene, Oregon, in 1989

From left: Terri's then-boyfriend Andy, Terri, Mom, and me in Boston in 1995

Serving kimchi to guests at the J-House, Dalian, China, in 2007

Me with some North Korean children after their performance in 2011, before my detainment

Smiling in Pyongyang during a group tour in 2012

Spending family time with Sophia and Natalie in Changchun, China, in 2012

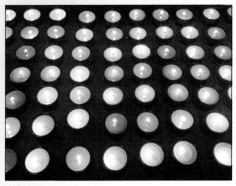

In August 2013, my family and friends in Seattle organized a prayer vigil for my release.

The posters they made and placed in the lobby showed a brief timeline.

A few of the colorful prayer cards people wrote for me. I loved seeing these.

This poster raised awareness of how many days I was in captivity.

281 days
imprisoned in North Korea

please help us
Bring Kenneth Home

Sign the petition: https://www.change.org/FreeKenNow

Send letters to Kenneth: letterforkennethbae@gmail.com

For more information and updates: www.freekennow.com

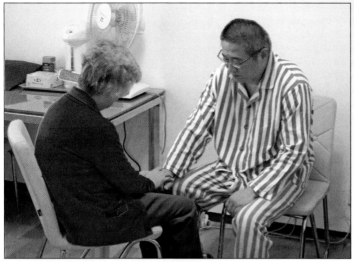

My mother visiting
me in North Korea
in October 2013

Choson Sinbo
filmed our reunion.

Receiving a special
pardon by the order
of Kim Jong Un
at a ceremony on
November 8, 2014

Hugging mom on the tarmac at the airport. So good to be home.

Speaking to the media at a press conference at the airport

With my mom and Terri's family at the airport

Arrival prayer with family. From left: Bobby Lee, mom, me, Eugene Cho, Ella, Caitlin.

My prayer was answered! Giving thanks and celebrating Thanksgiving with family in November 2014. From left: Andy, Terri, Jonathan, Natalie, Sophia, Lydia, me, Caitlin, Dad, mom, Ella.

Taking a vision trip to Cambodia with Lydia

Me and Lydia on the beach in Hawaii with my new Seahawks hat

Dad, mom, and me in Hawaii visiting Volcanoes National Park in 2015

Receiving a special welcome from the University of the Nations in Kona, Hawaii, in 2015

Reunited with my kids Natalie and Jonathan in Sedona, Arizona

Celebration and thank-you party with "Free Ken Now" volunteers in Seattle. From left: Derek Sciba, mom, Terri, me, Bobby Lee, John Thomas, Kelly Sadler, Euna Lee.

screen was filled with lots of static. The color faded in and out. I tried switching channels, but the central TV station was the only one I found. I let out a long sigh. Instead of the occasional foreign movie or outside program, I was stuck with the usual propaganda programs extolling the wonders of North Korea's leaders. I was too tired to care. All I wanted was to lie down.

At long last ten o'clock came, and the guard at my door told me I could go to sleep. I collapsed on my bed and passed out. Not even the light shining down on me bothered me.

I did not stir until the next morning around six. After a small breakfast I spent an hour reading my Bible, singing, and praying, before I was led back outside to spend another day working in the field. Just walking out there took all of my spiritual energy. My body ached, but my spirit ached even more. *If I am going to survive this, I have to put on the full armor of God*, I told myself.

When I reached the field, I took my hoe and started planting where I had left off the day before. While I dug I silently recited Ephesians 6:13–17. I went over each piece of God's armor and felt myself place it over my spirit. The belt of truth, the breastplate of righteousness, the helmet of salvation, and the shield of faith covered me. I looked at my hoe and imagined it to be the sword of the Spirit. As each piece went on, my strength grew. From that day on, I never left my room without first putting on the full armor of God to prepare me for the spiritual battles awaiting me.

My second day in the field was pretty much like my first, as was the third day and the fourth and on and on and on. The only exception was the day I spent spreading fertilizer instead of planting. I preferred planting. The fertilizer consisted of pig manure mixed with dried leaves and cut with water. I hauled it out into the field on the A-frame, trying to balance two bucketfuls of this smelly mixture. I spilled more than made it into the field. Eventually the guards told me to carry one bucket at a time.

I cannot describe the smell. It reeked of the most awful stink I've ever experienced.

I started singing more and more as I worked. I found it lifted my spirits and made the time go by much faster. Most days I sang praise songs. One afternoon I got so caught up in worshiping my Lord that a huge smile broke out on my face. I was hot. My back ached. My knees were sore. But in my spirit I was in the presence of God. Finally one of the guards yelled over at me, "Hey, 103, if you are the prisoner, why do you look like you are enjoying this more than we do? Stop it."

The Swedish ambassador came to visit me during my first week in the labor camp. "Help is on the way," he reassured me. "Your government is working to bring you home. Just hang in there. In the meantime, my office is doing everything it can to get you transferred to a hospital and out of this camp. Your mother mailed your medical records to us, and we forwarded them to the prison doctor. We hope to hear something soon."

He also brought me letters from home. My sister told me that she, my mother, and my wife had all written apology letters to the government of North Korea on my behalf. My sister and my son had also written letters to the secretary of state, John Kerry, pleading with him to get me home. My son even wrote President Obama asking him to intervene for me.

That first week a new visitor came to see me. He introduced himself as the camp political officer, the person responsible for ensuring the orthodoxy of the rank and file's political views. Each Saturday he came to the prison and conducted what is called *study hour*. In North Korea, study hour is like going to church, only instead of studying the Bible, people study and memorize Kim Jong Un's latest speech or something pulled from Kim Il Sung's or Kim Jong Il's writings.

Everyone in the prison had a military rank, and the political officer was no different. He was a colonel, which made him the same rank as the warden, although I was sure the political officer wielded more power. Unlike other high-ranking officials, he was thin and looked very sharp. He introduced himself as a Kim Il Sung University graduate, and he was very proud of that. He was soft-spoken and seemed to have a gentle personality.

The first time the political officer came to see me, he was on his best behavior. "How are you doing?" he asked. "How is your health? I understand you have some back problems. How is your back holding up? Do you need anything? Is there anything I can do for you?"

In later visits he kept up the Mr. Nice Guy tone, but his real motives started coming out. In one visit about a month after I had arrived at the camp, he asked me, "Do you want to become famous?"

I asked him what he meant.

"I can give you some books about our Great Leader, Kim Il Sung, and about juche. I think that if you read them and carefully consider what they say, you will want to convert to our side. When you do, I will make you very, very famous."

I laughed to myself. Here I was, in prison for being a missionary, and the political officer was doing mission work right in front of me. He was every bit the preacher I was, only his religion was juche.

"You know I am a Christian missionary and pastor," I replied.

"Yes. Of course I know that. That's what will make you so famous," the political officer said with a smile. "If you read the truth about our system, I believe you will see the light."

"I already have my God and my beliefs," I said.

"I know all about your beliefs," he said with a dismissive tone. "Why do you believe in a god who is not there, when you can believe in something real? You can believe in yourself and in the Leader."

"I am not interested in changing. Besides, I know all about juche. They gave me some books about it when I was in Pyongyang," I said.

"Just let me know if you are interested in learning more. I will bring you some books for you to study," he said, not wanting to take no for an answer.

The political officer came to see me at least once a week. We often talked about each other's version of truth. He said that he had learned about Christianity at the university, and he found it quite amusing to see people falling for such nonsense even in the twenty-first century. I told him that more than three out of four people in the world believe in some sort of higher power or supernatural being, and one out of three people in the world believes in Christianity. North Korea is the only country in the world whose people do not believe in supernatural gods but believe in the Leader as god and juche as their only doctrine. But the political officer was certain that what he believes is the only truth.

During his visits, the political officer also gave me little things that made life more bearable, including toilet paper. I wondered why he bothered, since toilet paper is a basic item the prison should have given me. I learned the answer when I ran out of the paper the political officer had brought to me. I asked the guards for more, and they brought me a roll of rough, brown paper that reminded me of the cheap paper towels in public bathrooms. Only then did I realize that I had been using the toilet paper enjoyed only by the ruling class and upper party members.

Converting to juche was never going to happen, but while I was in the detention center in Pyongyang, I had read many North Korean books, including Kim Il Sung's eight-volume memoir from his revolutionary days. Kim Il Sung wrote six of the books himself. Another writer put together the other two using Kim's notes. I read all eight while I was waiting for trial. I had seen the movie many, many times, so I thought I might as well read the books. I also read Kim Jong Il's book that outlines the entire juche system. The books gave me insight into the beliefs and worldviews of the North Korean people that I could not have gained otherwise. If I ever hoped to engage in an intelligent conversation with them about the one true God, I knew I needed to understand their system and their concept of God.

I had arrived at the labor camp on May 14. Just over a month later, in late June, the chief prosecutor came to see me.

"Well, it looks like your government doesn't care about you," he said.

"They don't act like they did back in 2009, when the two reporters were here. President Clinton came and took them home. I know, because I was the prosecutor in that case. But there is no Clinton this time, or anyone else. No one has come for you. Maybe no one comes because you are not a full American."

"What does that mean?" I asked. "I am an American citizen."

"Yes, but you are Asian. You are not white."

"The two reporters in 2009 were both Asian. I don't see how that matters."

"It matters," the prosecutor said, "because something is different. Perhaps you have not done enough to convince your government of the seriousness of your situation." He took out a stack of blank paper. "You must write more letters instructing your family to do more for you. You need to be very firm in your appeal. You need to let them know how desperate your situation is here. Otherwise, you will probably be here until I retire."

Isn't that the idea? I wondered. After all, the chief prosecutor was the one who had asked for a fifteen-year sentence.

This conversation made it very clear that he never intended for me to be there long. My arrest, conviction, and sentence struck me as a show of force put on to prove something to America and the world. Now more than ever, I did not believe I was going to have to stay there more than just a few more weeks. Every other American that had been detained in North Korea had been released in a few weeks to, at most, a few months. I knew my time was coming.

I still believed God's promise: he was going to bring me home without any harm coming to me or to anyone else. I clung to that promise like a lifeline.

I doubted a new set of letters would make much more difference than the last set, but I wrote them anyway: one to my wife, one to my mother, and one to my sister. So many letters had already been written to the highest levels of the United States government, including the president himself. I didn't think one more was going to push everyone to do more than they already were. But, if nothing else, the letters at least let my family know I was okay. I knew they wanted to hear from me. They all had to be very worried about me.

I finished the letters, and the chief prosecutor took them to mail them. That night I endured more television propaganda extolling the virtues and wonders of the Great Leader. The next day I woke up at six and was back out in the fields by eight.

This was my new routine.

This was my new life.

I did not know how long it might last. At least it couldn't last longer than fifteen years. I prayed it wouldn't last fifteen more days.

FIFTEEN ———————————————————————

THE WHOLE WORLD
NOW KNOWS

"Give thanks to the LORD Almighty,
for the LORD is good;
his love endures forever."

—JEREMIAH 33:11

FROM THE DAY I was arrested, I had not wanted any press coverage of my case. I hoped to resolve everything as quietly as possible, so that later on I could return to North Korea and resume my work. Looking back, I realize that was never going to be possible, but I held out that hope all the way through my trial. In my letters and phone calls, I asked my family not to go to the news networks. There were stories in the media about my arrest, and Bill Richardson's visit to North Korea grabbed a lot of headlines a few months before my trial. However, my family stayed quiet. They didn't do interviews or make public statements about me.

However, once my conviction and sentence went public, so did my family. Today I am very glad they did.

North Korea actually broke the news of my conviction through their official state news agency. The story was picked up by every major news outlet, including all the cable news networks, the BBC, and the *New York Times*. Commentators jumped in and said the sentence was a ploy to force America to open talks that would recognize North Korea as a legitimate nuclear power. I was now a bargaining chip, they said.

The US government refused to play along. A State Department spokesman, Patrick Ventrell, held a news conference in which he called on the DPRK to grant me amnesty and my immediate release.

The day after my trial, my sister, Terri, made her first of several appearances on CNN's *Anderson Cooper 360*. "We just pray, and ask for leaders of both nations to, please, just see him as one man, caught in between," Terri said to Anderson. "He's a father to three children, and we just ask that he be allowed to come home."[1]

Terri became the face of the efforts to bring me home and my voice to the world. She wrote an editorial for the *Seattle Times*, reached out to high-profile officials who could help—including President Carter, President Clinton, Secretary Clinton, and Secretary Albright—and did interviews with everyone who asked. In 2014 she twice visited Washington, DC, and even had a meeting at the White House. She spoke with National Security Council members and visited with under-secretary Wendy Sherman at the State Department. In another trip, she pleaded my case to Secretary Kerry.

Terri wasn't the only one who spoke out about me. My family also started a grassroots effort to bring me home. My son, Jonathan, created a petition at Change.org calling on North Korea to grant me amnesty. All together 177,552 people signed the petition.[2] Bobby Lee, a friend of mine from college, created a website and a Facebook group to raise awareness of my case. Later, Terri's college roommate, Laura Choi, and her husband, Isaac, took over maintenance of the website. They posted all the latest news about me and asked people to contact the State Department, Congress, the White House, and anyone else they could think of to urge them to bring me home. Euna Lee and Laura Ling started a letter-writing campaign for me, because they remembered the letters they had received had sustained them during their four and a half months of captivity in North Korea.

Even basketball Hall of Famer Dennis Rodman got in on the act. He read about my story in the *Seattle Times* and then tweeted, "I'm calling on the Supreme Leader of North Korea or as I call him 'Kim', to do me a solid and cut Kenneth Bae loose."[3] I'll talk more about Dennis Rodman later on. I've never met him, and he said some things later in my imprisonment that really caught my family off guard and hurt them, but in May 2013, I think my family and friends welcomed anyone speaking out for me. If it was going to get me home, they were all for it.

Of course, I didn't know any of this was going on. I couldn't get cable news in the labor camp, nor did I or anyone else have access to the Internet. The Swedish ambassador told me my sister had appeared on CNN calling for my release, but that was all I knew. For me, the growing media frenzy might as well have taken place on another planet. I remained prisoner 103. I spent my days working in the soybean field and my nights reading while the television bombarded me with stories of the glories of the Great Leader.

The incessant propaganda made me feel even worse than I already did, and I felt pretty awful. The prison doctor came to see me once a week. He always asked how I felt, which I answered honestly. I told him my back hurt, and I was losing a lot of weight, and my entire body ached. No matter what I said, he always replied, "What did you expect? This is a labor camp. Of course your back is hurting. Work will make you feel better."

On most of his visits he gave me some of the medicines I needed, but not all of them. A couple of months in, he tested my blood sugar levels and announced to me, "You are normal. You do not have diabetes anymore. See, I told you work would heal you." If my diabetes had improved, it had to be because of the weight loss. I was not sure how much weight I had lost, but I knew my clothes had become very loose.

I was also starting to feel the effects of my lack of sleep. The light that never went out was bad enough, but it was nothing compared to the heat and the insects. The prison was very hot, so the guards opened the windows, which did not have screens. Throughout the day my room filled up with flies, gnats, and mosquitoes. At night before I went to sleep, I closed my window, but that only made the room hotter without solving my insect problem. So many bugs came in during the day that I spent most of the evening trying to kill them so I could try to sleep. Even after I killed what I could, more bugs flew in through the cracks around the window, drawn by the light shining in my room. Their incessant buzzing and dive-bombing made my nights miserable.

One afternoon in late June, I was out in the field, dripping with sweat, when I noticed a film crew taping me. The chief prosecutor was with them.

"Keep working," he said. "Do not pay attention to the camera."

After a few minutes of filming, the cameraman put down his camera and went inside. The prosecutor took me by the arm and said, "Come with me, 103."

He led me back to my room, where a camera was already set up on a tripod. A woman sat in a chair nearby, waiting for me. The prosecutor introduced us. "This is a reporter from *Choson Sinbo*, and she is here to interview you," he said. *Choson Sinbo* is a pro–North Korean newspaper that operates out of Tokyo, Japan. The name literally means, "The People's Korea." "She will ask questions, and you must be truthful. We plan on releasing the video to Western news agencies. Maybe then your government will do something to secure your release."

The chief prosecutor told me to be truthful, but I knew I was to say only that which the North Koreans considered true. If I complained about my treatment in any way, I would suffer.

"Do you want me to change into clean clothes first?" I asked.

"No. You are fine," the prosecutor said. "The reporter is going to ask about your physical conditions and how you are treated. Make sure you tell her how well you have been taken care of here."

This was a true statement in the prosecutor's mind. Compared to the average North Korean serving time in a labor camp, I was in a four-star resort.

"You must also ask your government to get busy for you," he reminded me. "Perhaps they have forgotten you. This interview should jog their memory."

"I understand," I said. I thought for a moment about what I could and could not say. I also glanced at my arms. My prison uniform was filthy and ill fitting. I had filled it out a month earlier; now it hung on me. My head had also been freshly shaved a day or two earlier. I hated it when I got a new haircut. It was a reminder that I was not going anywhere soon.

What will my family think when they see me? I wondered.

"Mr. Bae," the reporter started. "How is prison life? Is it bearable for you?"

"Yes," I said, "life is bearable. I mainly work on the farm from morning until dinnertime, eight hours a day. I've never farmed before, so this is all new to me. But the people here are very considerate, and they do not work me too hard. However, my health is not in the best condition, so there are some difficulties. But everyone here is considerate and generous, and we have doctors here, so I'm getting regular checkups." I did not mention that the checkups mainly served as a way for the doctor to tell me that I would feel better if I worked harder. "Although my health is not good, I am being patient and coping well. And I hope that with the help of the North Korean government and the United States, I will be released soon."

"In your trial, you refused the DPRK offer of an attorney to represent you. Why did you do this?" the reporter asked. She read the question from a piece of paper. The question seemed designed to show the world how they had respected my rights and had given me a fair trial.

"I admitted to the charges," I said, "so I thought that it wasn't really necessary to have a defense lawyer during the trial. I admitted my crime and apologized for it." I did not mention anything about how I couldn't meet with my lawyer ahead of time. Given the circumstances, I didn't think such details were going to do me much good.

"Do you have anything to say to the North Korean government and your own government?" she asked.

"I know what I did is not easily forgivable, but I hope that things will work out so that I can be with family again soon. The Fourth of July is my father's seventieth birthday, so I hope I can be with him on this very special day. So my hope is that North Korea will forgive, and the United States will try harder to get me out speedily. I am asking for their help."

I paused. Thinking about my father's birthday reminded me of everything else I had missed. Emotion overcame me.

"I am an only son . . . My father . . ." I could barely get the words out. "I really hope to go to congratulate him on his birthday."

After the interview I went back to work in the field. My father and the rest of my family filled my thoughts. I hoped seeing me would comfort them. Even though we had spoken on the phone a couple of times, there is nothing like seeing someone to reassure you that he or she is all right. I also hoped it might move North Korea and America to negotiate my release.

Weeks passed after my interview, and nothing happened. My first soybean plants started coming up. With nothing left to plant, I spent my days pulling weeds by hand.

One day in early July, the warden came out to me. "You are too slow!" he complained. "If our people were working on this field, we would have been finished a long time ago."

"I'm doing the best I can, sir," I said.

"Your best isn't very good. Look at our field over there," the warden said, pointing to the field where the guards worked when they weren't standing over me. "Do you see how much further along our plants are than yours? Do you see how beautiful our field is? That's what yours should look like."

I thought of reminding him that they had several people working their field while I was all on my own. I also thought of mentioning how my field was on the side of a hill while theirs was down in the valley. Instead I said, "That's a pretty field, but for the plants to grow really well, you need help from heaven."

"What are you talking about?" the warden said.

"You need help from heaven, from God, to send the rain and the sunshine and everything plants need to produce a large harvest," I said.

The warden scoffed. "Heaven?" he laughed. "We have our juche agriculture system given to us by Kim Il Sung. As long as we follow his methods, we'll always have a great harvest. We don't need any god to help us." His voice rose as he said this. He was really angry that I had mentioned God and questioned the power of juche.

That night thunder and flashes of lightning woke me up. I heard rain pouring down. Then I heard some sort of commotion from inside the building. People were yelling, and I heard footsteps running up and down the hallway and the outside door slamming. I was too tired to get up and look out my window. Instead I rolled over and went back to sleep.

The next morning I saw the warden go past my room, visibly upset. "What happened?" I asked.

"There was a flood last night. The entire bean field is underwater. It's all lost," he said. This was a huge blow because these beans were supposed to feed the guards and the rest of the staff.

When I went outside, I noticed everything was not lost. The guards' field was washed away—but my field was fine. I felt a little like the Israelites when the plagues hit Egypt but left them alone.

I smiled and prayed to myself, *Lord, you are really humorous. You sure made your point here!*

I needed this reminder of God's faithfulness, because June and July were very hard months for me. The days were so hot that the guards quit standing around me in a triangle. Instead, they found a shady place and watched me from a distance. I tried striking up conversations with them, but they were not open to talking, except to make sure I knew they were in charge.

One day when it rained, I worked inside, scrubbing the floors by hand with a scrub brush. I worked on my hands and knees, like Cinderella. I dropped the scrub brush in a bucket of water, pulled it out, and scrubbed part of the floor. Then I used a towel to wipe it clean and dry. One of the young guards came by after I'd done about a third of the hallway near my room. "You call this clean?" he yelled. "This is not quality work. Do this again!"

"Okay," I said.

He spun around on his boots. "How are you supposed to address me, 103? Is that how you are supposed to address me? You say it again correctly this time!"

"Yes, sir," I said.

"Did you have permission to speak, 103?" he snapped back.

"I am sorry. Excuse me, teacher. May I speak, please?" I said, still on the floor.

"Stand up when you speak to me," he said.

I stood up and repeated, "Excuse me, teacher. May I speak, please?" Having to call him *teacher* and *sir* felt very strange because I was old enough to be the guard's father.

"Yes, you may speak, 103."

"Yes, teacher, I will scrub the floor again," I said.

"That's better, 103. Now, get to work."

This young guard seemed to enjoy finding fault with everything I did. He had the kind of personality where everything had to be done perfectly, and I never measured up. He was also very much a rule follower.

In the beginning he made it clear he did not like me. "You are Korean, but you work for the US government. You are a spy, aren't you? How dare you do that to our country?"

I never argued or tried to defend myself. I knew my words could never convince him I was something other than what he'd already decided I was. Instead I tried very hard to do my work well and to do it with the right attitude. I believed that if they could see a difference in me, then their hearts might soften.

Despite the hope I had expressed in the *Choson Sinbo* interview, my father's birthday came and went, and I was no closer to going home.

My clothes kept getting looser. Every day I worked my field while the guards watched from the shade.

One of the older guards asked me one day, "How can you live in America? It is so violent."

"It isn't violent," I said. "Most places are perfectly safe."

"How can you say it is safe when so many people get shot and the women are raped?" I knew where these questions were coming from. North Korean news programs pull the worst crime footage from the States and show it over and over, telling viewers this is everyday life in America.

"There are a few places that are dangerous, but most of the country is not that way. When I lived in the city of St. Louis, in the middle of the country, I never even locked my doors," I replied. I mentioned St. Louis even though I knew he had no idea what I was talking about.

"What kind of place did you live in?" the guard asked. "Did you have an apartment or a house or what?"

"I had an apartment in St. Louis, but we owned our own house when we lived in Atlanta. And I owned cars in both places."

The other two guards who were listening to the conversation reacted as if I had just lost my mind. "How can you own a house and a car?" one asked in a tone that made it clear he believed this to be impossible.

"In America we have a thing called credit," I said. "You buy the car and take it home, and then you pay for it a little every month."

"How do people pay for things? No one has jobs over there. Ninety percent of the people live on the streets," the first guard said.

"No, that's not true. Most people own their own cars and homes, at least the ones who want to," I said.

"The government supplies us with all we want," the third guard chimed in. "They build us houses and give them to us to live in." The other two gave him a little look as if to tell him to shut up. I knew what he was saying was no longer true. Years earlier most people had lived in government-provided housing, but no longer. Now people had to make their own way, with average people unable to afford their own homes. Generations now shared the same small houses and apartments.

"Anyway, enough talk," the guard said. "Get back to work, 103. You're slow enough without wasting time talking."

July passed. I had been depressed when I could not be with my father on his birthday, but now my own birthday had arrived. I went out in the field on August 1 just as I did every day. It was really hard to act as if this were just another day. On my last birthday, back in Dandong, my staff threw a surprise party for me, with cake and everything else. Here, no one knew or cared that it was my birthday. I shouldn't have cared either, but there's something about birthdays that always makes me sentimental.

I had been out in the field about two hours when the deputy warden told me to come back inside. I had no idea what was going on. Perhaps *Choson Sinbo* was back for another interview.

I walked to my room and found the political officer there waiting for me.

"Happy birthday," he said. "I'm sorry I didn't get here earlier, because here, you don't have to work on your birthday. You have the rest of the day off."

"Thank you," I said.

"I brought you something," he said. He brought out some instant ramen noodles, a substitute for the noodles that Koreans traditionally eat on their birthdays. He also had bread and soda. "I hope you enjoy your day today. I know your family will be thinking about you and you them, so I wanted to make sure you got a little comfort."

The warden had walked in while the political officer made his presentation. "You know," the warden said, "he bought all this with his own money."

I was touched that he did this for me. However, I wasn't quite sure what his motives might have been. Perhaps the political officer was trying to convert me through his acts of kindness. Whatever his motives, I was very thankful that I did not have to work outside on such a hot summer day. I enjoyed the treats and the day off.

A few days later the prison doctor came in for his weekly visit. It was the same routine: He asked how I was feeling. I went through my list of ailments. Then he always said, "What do you expect? You are in a labor camp."

However, on Saturday, August 3, 2013, the doctor actually seemed to listen to me. The chief prosecutor had come with him, but I don't think he had any influence on the doctor. After all, it was the chief prosecutor who had me sent to the camp even after I failed my medical exam.

The prison doctor asked me how I felt. I told him, "I know I've lost a lot of weight, and I get dizzy a lot."

The chief prosecutor spoke up. "Do you think we should check him into the hospital for a thorough examination?"

The doctor scrunched up his forehead as he thought. "That may not be a bad idea. There's only so much I can do here."

"All right," the prosecutor said. "I will make the arrangements."

At first I thought this was an honest conversation, but then I thought about something the chief prosecutor had said on an earlier visit. He had made an offhand comment about how most prisoners stay in this labor camp for only three months. My three months were up. Maybe something else was going on.

I did not want to get my hopes up. I told myself that I was just going to the hospital for a few tests and then I would be right back, but I couldn't help but wonder if I was about to go home.

On Monday morning the guard told me to gather all my things together. *This could be it,* I told myself.

That afternoon the chief prosecutor came to my room. "Time to go," he said.

I looked around my room. *Good-bye, room 3. I hope I never see you again.*

The warden, deputy warden, and the guards all came by my room as I left. "Good-bye," I said to them.

"Good-bye, 103," the warden said. The way he said it sounded really final, like a final good-bye.

I walked out to the waiting minivan with the prosecutor and took one last look at the labor camp. Finally, my nightmare was coming to an end. I never thought I would see that place again.

GOING HOME?

"Do not let your hearts be troubled. You believe in God; believe also in me."

—JOHN 14:1

DURING THE DRIVE to the hospital from the labor camp, I once again was placed between guards in the backseat of the curtained minivan and was forced to ride with my head down between my knees. They wanted to keep my destination a secret, but I recognized it the moment I stepped out.

They took me to Chin-Sun Hospital, also known as Friendship Hospital. Located near the diplomatic compound in the center of Pyongyang, the hospital cares only for foreign patients, mainly Russians and Chinese diplomats. The building reminded me of a small-town hospital. It wasn't very big at all. There were three floors in the main building, with another couple of smaller buildings attached to it.

The chief prosecutor led me inside. Two guards from the labor camp walked behind us. We walked down a couple of hallways before making a right turn, which led to a pair of rooms at the end of a dead-end hall.

"This is where you will stay, 103," the prosecutor said to me, pointing to the room on the right.

The moment I walked into my room I felt rejuvenated. The hospital had air-conditioning, which felt like heaven after three months in a hot, insect-filled room. The room itself was a VIP suite and was divided into three sections. It had a separate living area, including a large sofa, with a connecting door to the bedroom. It also had a bathroom with a real bathtub and a regular toilet. (In the camp I had to use a squat-style toilet instead of a Western one.) In addition to the bed, the room also had a refrigerator and a dining table with a couple of chairs. There was also a television. I dreaded seeing it there, but I was also happy to have something that connected me to the outside world. Even though I was in a VIP suite, my privacy was limited. The guards kept an eye on me through a large window in the door.

A couple of nurses were already in my room. A fresh set of pajama-like clothes were laid out on the bed for me. I was happy to see them. My prison clothes were stained and didn't smell too good, even though I washed them when I bathed. I went into the bathroom and changed clothes.

When I came out, my doctor was waiting for me. She was in her fifties and was very thin and petite, with a warm smile. "The actual tests will not start until the morning," she said. "I don't want you to eat breakfast or anything else tomorrow until we are finished. Don't worry," she said. "We'll bring you some food as soon as we are finished."

The next morning, nurses came into my room to draw blood and take a urine sample. They took me to another room, where they did an ultrasound on my gallbladder, and to a third room, where I had X-rays taken of my back. I was also poked and prodded, and I went through a whole gamut of tests. The medical staff was very thorough.

Later in the day, my doctor gave me the results. "We found a problem with your back. We also found gallstones, and your prostate is enlarged," she said. I was not surprised, since I had had these conditions before I entered North Korea back in November. "And we determined you are suffering from malnutrition."

That diagnosis did not surprise me. I had lost more than fifty pounds since November.

"What about my diabetes?" I asked. I did not believe the prison doctor's claim that it was gone.

"All the tests for diabetes came back negative. It seems you no longer have it," she said. "We will start treatments for malnutrition right away. We should have you as good as new very soon."

The chief prosecutor came to see me right after the doctor gave me the diagnosis. "You're going to be here for a while," he said. "Get some rest and get treated, and then that's it." I wasn't sure what he meant by that. I hoped "that's it" meant, "That will be the end of your time here, and you're going to go home."

The treatment for malnutrition mainly consisted of nutrient injections into my IV. They also gave me some supplements. However, aside from aspirin for my back pain, they didn't treat my gallstones or back. I thought they probably wanted to get my weight up so that I might look healthy when I got to go home.

The chief prosecutor must have meant what he said about rest, because I was allowed to lie down as much as I wanted. Back in the labor camp, I had to sit upright in a chair whenever I was not working out in the field. Not here. Here they treated me like any other patient, not a criminal. I could lie down or sleep however much I needed.

Unfortunately, I still had to watch propaganda on the television from the moment the channels started broadcasting until they went off the air. There was no escaping that. They also kept my door locked at all times. The guards had to open it with a key for doctors and nurses to come in, and the guards stayed in the room with them until they were finished with me.

Mr. Lee came to see me not long after I arrived. "From now on I am going to be the one checking on you," he told me, which made me feel a little better. I decided to call him Mr. Sympathy in my head, because he was the only North Korean official I had met during my time there who actually seemed to care about me. I enjoyed talking with him.

I adjusted to life in the hospital very quickly. I spent the first two weeks in my room resting, an IV in my arm several hours a day. One thing struck me as a little odd. Sometimes when my door was open, I could hear a dog barking. The first time I heard it I thought, *What kind of hospital is this? Do they treat both dogs and people here?*

The Swedish ambassador came to see me about a week after I arrived at the hospital. Once again he assured me the United States was doing everything it could to secure my release. I listened closely to try to detect any extra enthusiasm in his voice, something to indicate the efforts to bring me home were getting close. But he just told me efforts were under way, which was still encouraging to me. At least I had not been forgotten.

His deputy, John Svensson, came to see me a couple of weeks later to tell me he was going to travel to the United States in early September to discuss my case with the State Department. That got my hopes up even more.

Choson Sinbo showed up for another interview on the same day the ambassador came to see me. They set up a video camera in my room and asked me a series of questions: "Why did the North Korean government send you to the hospital? Why are you here? How is your health now?"

I went through the list of my ailments. "Mainly," I told them, "I am being treated for malnutrition. My hand is also numb, and I have shooting pains in my leg. That's why they put me in the hospital."

Then the reporter asked, "Do you have anything to say to the United States government?"

I had to say the same thing I said before. "Please, do anything you can," I pleaded. I knew the entire interview was designed to put more pressure on the United States. It was the DPRK's way of saying, "We sent one of yours to the labor camp because he deserved it. Now, we are treating him in one of our best hospitals as a humanitarian gesture. However, if you don't do something, we will send him back to the camp." They didn't say that in so many words, but that was the real message they wanted to get across through *Choson Sinbo*.

After two weeks of IVs and rest, I was allowed to go out to the hallway and get some exercise. A guard escorted me out for the walk. I recognized him as one of the guards from the labor camp. We walked past the room right next to mine. I glanced through the door and noticed another guard sitting in a chair. Both beds had clothes and books piled on top.

"Is that where you're staying?" I asked.

"Yes," he replied. "Three of us rotate shifts to guard your door. Don't even think about trying to escape." He tried to sound tough, as usual, but his heart didn't really seem to be in it. By this point he knew I posed no threat.

"Don't worry about me escaping. I am in the safest and the most comfortable place in North Korea. Besides, where could I run to?"

He nodded and said, "That's true."

The guard and I walked down the hall, which was about twenty yards long. When we reached the main hallway, I turned around and went back toward our rooms. The prison officials wanted to keep my presence in the hospital a secret from anyone else who happened to be staying there.

As we walked I noticed a set of windows on the interior side of the hallway that looked out on an inner courtyard. I was looking out the window very closely, trying to figure out exactly what was in there, when all of a sudden, this large, hairy, English shepherd leaped up on the glass and started barking at me. I nearly jumped out of my skin.

"Hey, buddy. What are you doing here?" I said to the dog.

He kept barking. As I walked farther down the hall, the dog dropped down and then jumped up on the next window, and the next and the next, barking the whole time, until we passed the courtyard.

Over the next several days, I took more and more walks past the courtyard windows. The first few days the dog jumped up and barked at me. "Hey, pal, why are you barking? I see you. I'm paying attention to you," I told him.

Before long the dog stopped barking. Instead, he jumped up on the window and let out a little yap to get my attention. When I talked to him, his tail wagged back and forth as if he were really glad to see me. I had made my first friend.

I never saw anyone inside the courtyard playing with him, although from time to time I saw someone in there feeding him.

Talking to the dog each day became the high point of my walks. It was as though he were looking for me. Maybe I was his only friend as well.

About a month after I arrived at the hospital, I woke up and something was different. The first thing I noticed was that all three guards were on duty, not the usual one or two. Not only that, all three wore their full uniforms. Normally, all the guards dressed very casually to keep from standing out in the hospital. Today they wore their full military uniforms, with belts that came down across their chests. They also wore their hats, as if they had to go to some official function.

Then Mr. Lee came in and said, "Get ready. Someone is coming to see you." I had no idea who that might be.

A few minutes later a camera crew came into my room, followed by a couple of North Korean officials. Then a few more officials joined them. Everyone seemed really worked up.

All of a sudden, the door opened, and two tall, distinguished-looking American men came into my room. After having seen almost exclusively Korean people for nearly a year, I thought the Americans looked huge.

One of the men crossed the room and hugged me. "I work for the White House," he said. "I'm with the National Security Council. The president sent me here to check on you and find out how you are really doing. That's also why I brought the doctor with me." He gestured to the other American.

I nearly burst into tears I was so glad to see these two men. *Finally, for the first time in a year, I am seeing fellow Americans, and they're here to take me home.*

"Thank you so much for coming," I said. We spoke English, of course. I saw the North Korean translators making notes and whispering to the other men in the room. Mr. Lee stood off to one side. He spoke some English, but I wasn't sure how much of this conversation he might understand.

"How are you really doing, Kenneth?" the man from the White House asked. "Physically and mentally."

"Well, I'm okay, considering," I said. "I've been in the hospital for nearly a month now, so I'm a lot better now than I was when they first brought me here. They've fed me better here than in the labor camp, and they are also giving me supplements through my IV. So I'm a lot stronger."

"How's your back? I know you've had a lot of trouble with that," the doctor said.

"Not working out in the field has made it feel better. I even get some physical therapy." That therapy consisted of one of the female therapists walking on my back for ten minutes. It felt pretty awful, and I thought it probably made my back worse, not better. But I did not mention that fact, since everything I said was being closely monitored.

"How is the food?" the representative from the White House inquired.

"The food is okay. I have been treated fairly."

"What are your symptoms?" the doctor asked. I went down the entire list for him. The doctor took notes. "And what are they doing for you?" he asked. I gave him a rundown of my treatment, which didn't take long.

"Kenneth," the other American said, "I want to assure you that getting you home is a high priority for us. We're doing everything we can. But your situation is very complex. We're trying to get you home, but it is really difficult to get you out of here. The fact that your health is not horrible is a good thing in light of the delays."

My heart sank. I wasn't going anywhere today. It sounded as though if I had been dying, they could have cut a deal right away. But because my health had improved, I was stuck here.

Before I could say anything, the North Korean minder cut off the conversation. "No more. It's finished. You must go."

The two Americans stood. "It was an honor to meet you, and bless you," the doctor said. He gave me a hug.

The other man did as well. "Don't worry, Kenneth. We're going to get you out of here and get you home. Please be patient. However, keep this visit to yourself for now."

"I will," I said. The fact that a White House representative had come all this way for a five-minute top-secret visit told me that I was a priority for my country. But it also crushed my hopes of a quick release.

The two men left. I sat down on my bed, dejected. I thought their arrival was my ticket out of here. Instead, the only certain release date I had was May 1, 2028, when my fifteen years were up. The thought depressed me.

Only a few minutes after they left, the two men suddenly returned. *Yes!* I thought. *I am leaving!* Instead the White House representative said, "The North Korean government gave us permission to take a photo of you. I think your family will be excited to get this, don't you?"

"Oh, yes, definitely," I said.

"Smile," he said. So I did.

I later learned my family never saw this photograph. I can only assume it was actually meant for the White House, to assure them that I was okay.

As soon as they were out the door, Mr. Lee returned. "Tell me, what did they ask and what did you say?" Apparently his English was not as good as he let on.

"They just wanted to know about my health," I said.

"And that's all?"

"Yes, that's all."

Mr. Lee seemed satisfied, but I was not. *Just be patient,* I told myself. *It won't be long now.*

SEVENTEEN

I Am a Missionary

"You did not choose me, but I chose you and appointed you so that you might go and bear fruit—fruit that will last."

—JOHN 15:16

A FEW DAYS after the secret visit, I received a letter from my mother. She included copies of two statements from the US State Department. The first said the DPRK had granted permission to special ambassador Robert King to come to North Korea to negotiate my release. I liked the sound of that. According to the letter, he was supposed to arrive in Pyongyang on August 30, 2013. I received this letter in mid-September and had not yet seen nor heard from the ambassador.

The second statement explained why. The day before Ambassador King was to travel from Japan to North Korea, the DPRK rescinded his invitation. Apparently, the fact that he considered flying in on a military plane upset them. I guess they viewed the plane as a threat and an insult. In addition, on August 28, the US military had sent B-52 bombers into South Korea from Guam as part of a joint military exercise with South Korea. North Korea perceived this as a great threat. Whatever the reason, the bottom line was that the ambassador was not coming.

No one was coming.

I was no closer to going home than I was back in November, when I was first arrested.

After reading the two statements from the State Department, I read my mother's letter. "You need to have faith, like Daniel's friends when they faced the fiery furnace," she wrote. "Remember, when the king threatened to throw them into the fire they said to him, 'The God we serve is able to deliver us from it, and he will deliver us from Your Majesty's hand. But even if he does not, we want you to know, Your Majesty, that we will not serve your gods or worship the image of gold you have set up' (Daniel 3:17–18). You must have the same faith now, my son. God is able to deliver you. But if he does not bring you home, you must continue to stand for him in your chains."

As I read my mother's letter, it hit me: God might not *want* me to go home. It might be his will for me to stay in North Korean custody. For nearly a year I had prayed, *God, rescue me.* What if his answer was no?

I'd been counting the days. I had made so many thirty-day calendars and had marked off each passing day as if I knew God planned on taking me home before I got to the end. Every time they cut my nails and my hair, I had made myself believe that it would be the last time before going home. I had pleaded with my government to do something for me. My family had written letters to President Obama and to Secretary of State Kerry, even to Kim Jong Un himself. It wasn't like their letters hadn't worked. Secretary of State Kerry had sent Ambassador King to bring me home, but the North Koreans had refused to let him enter the country. President Obama had sent one of his National Security Council members on a secret mission to bring me home, but it had failed as well.

Two failed rescue attempts in a week, I thought. *Two in a week! But I am no closer to going home. Oh, God, is this really what you want? How can you possibly want to leave me here, so far from home, separated from everyone I love, in a place that refuses to acknowledge you even exist?*

I went to bed that night really depressed and woke up the next morning the same way. *How, God?* I prayed, *How could you leave me here? You promised to rescue me and bring me home.*

From the time of my arrest I had meditated on all the promises of rescue in the Bible, especially in the psalms. *Does it mean God doesn't love me if he doesn't rescue me?* I wondered.

I reread the letters I'd received from home, letters from my wife, my mother, my sister, and my children. The letters made them seem close and yet so much farther away. *Is this the only way they are going to be able to know me for the next fifteen years? Is this the only contact I am going to get to have with everyone I love?*

I went back over the lines in my mother's last letter. "You are going to have to have the faith of Daniel's friends," she had said.

Am I that strong? Can I do what they did? Can I keep trusting in God, even if the worst-case scenario comes true?

For an entire week I wrestled with these questions. I prayed and prayed and asked God for wisdom and strength. My mood jumped between depressed and not quite as depressed. I sang sad songs, like the old Elvis tune "Are You Lonesome Tonight?" and Eric Carmen's "All by Myself." To be honest, I really started feeling sorry for myself.

Finally, on September 24, 2013, I got down on my knees on my bed and I prayed, *Lord, you know my heart. You know what I want, but not my will but yours be done. You know I want to go home, but if you want me to stay, I will stay. I give up my right to go home. I surrender it to you. Please, take care of my wife and my children and my parents. Please take care of them while you keep me here. If this is where you want me to be, okay. I embrace that as your will.*

Peace came over me as a weight lifted off my shoulders. God's Spirit filled the room and reminded me of my calling.

"I am a missionary," I said. "Lord, I am a missionary, and this is the mission field you have given me. Use me."

The moment I stopped praying, *God, save me*, and instead prayed, *God, use me*, I felt free. I was still in a North Korean hospital as a prisoner. I still faced fifteen years of hard labor once I was released from the hospital, but I was suddenly fine with all that. God wanted me in North Korea. God had called me here. He had a purpose for my being a prisoner.

I didn't know it then, but I still had more than a year of imprisonment in front of me. That didn't matter. The only thing that mattered was I was where God wanted me to be at the very moment he needed me to be here, and I love him. If I truly loved him, I would obey him. In light of all of this, there was truly only one thing I could pray: *God, use me.*

<hr />

Coming to peace with the possibility that God wanted me to stay imprisoned in North Korea for the foreseeable future did not mean I never again struggled with being there. The truth is, I had good days and I had bad days. Some days I welcomed this assignment; others I was so homesick that the thought of spending even another day in the Pyongyang hospital or, God forbid, back in the labor camp made me sick to my stomach. Those were the days I had to rely on the promise found in 2 Corinthians 12:9: "My grace is sufficient for you, for my power is made perfect in weakness." I felt very weak, but God's strength was enough.

I had two books with me that really helped me through these tough times. My wife, Lydia, sent me a copy of Rick Warren's *The Purpose Driven Life*. God used the entire book to speak to me during my imprisonment, but he especially used a couple of chapters to encourage me while I wrestled with embracing my role as a missionary in chains.

One day I felt very homesick. I wanted to see my wife. I wanted to see my kids. I wanted to see my mom and my sister and my dad. I just wanted to be home. Then I read day 36 of *The Purpose Driven Life*, a chapter called "Made for a Mission." It said:

> To fulfill your mission will require that you abandon your agenda and accept God's agenda for your life. You can't just "tack it on" to all the other things you'd like to do with your life. You must say, like Jesus, *"Father, . . . I want your will, not mine."* You yield your rights, expectations, dreams, plans, and ambitions to him. . . . You hand God a blank

I AM A MISSIONARY

sheet with your name signed at the bottom and tell him to fill in the details.[1]

That's what I had to do. I prayed again, *I yield my right to go home. I yield my right to be released. I accept your agenda as your will for my life.*

This wasn't an easy prayer to pray. I had my share of "Why me?" moments. God used another part of *The Purpose Driven Life* to help me through those. Day 25 is titled "Transformed by Trouble." Right in the middle of this chapter, I read:

> God could have kept Joseph out of jail, kept Daniel out of the lion's den, kept Jeremiah from being tossed into a slimy pit, kept Paul from being shipwrecked three times, and kept the three Hebrew young men from being thrown into a blazing furnace—but he didn't. He let those problems happen, and every one of those persons was drawn closer to God as a result.[2]

I added my name to the list. God could have kept me from getting arrested. He could have blinded the eyes of the border patrol agents who seized the external hard drive. Or he could have reminded me to look in my suitcase before I left the hotel in Yanji. God could have easily moved the agents in Rason to immediately deport me, or he could move Kim Jong Un to simply let me go now. Proverbs 21:1 says, "In the LORD's hand the king's heart is a stream of water that he channels toward all who please him." That includes Kim Jong Un's heart.

Yes, God could have done all of these things, but he chose not to. Instead, he chose to leave me there for the foreseeable future.

Another book I read helped me understand the reason. Lydia also sent me Kyle Idleman's book *Not a Fan: Becoming a Completely Committed Follower of Jesus.* He told the story of a group of missionaries who wanted to reach the inhabitants of an island just off of Suriname, in South America. Most of the people on the island were slaves. The plantation owners did not allow their slaves to talk with anyone except other slaves.

The missionaries tried to come up with a way to reach the slaves, but nothing worked. Finally they sold themselves into slavery so they could reach the slaves.[3]

When I read this story, my imprisonment made sense. I had entertained the idea of spending a couple of years in Pyongyang to try to reach average North Koreans, but that plan would never have worked. My contact with them would have been limited and every conversation monitored. What better way, then, to reach average North Koreans than to actually live with them as they went about their work and their day-to-day lives? But to do that I had to be a prisoner. That was the only way to reach the guards and prosecutors and the doctors and nurses at the hospital.

I was a missionary on assignment from God. Every morning I looked myself in the eye in the mirror and repeated, "I am a missionary. That's why I am here."

However, something else occurred to me as I made this transition. When I had prayed constantly for God to save me, the only person I had thought about was me. I wanted to show Jesus to my captors, but I wasn't nearly as concerned about them as I was about myself. Once I saw my imprisonment as God's will for my life, I started to see the people around me the way God saw them. Before, I felt depressed because I was trapped and had no hope. But that's exactly what the average North Korean faces every day! They are trapped, and they have no hope.

My self-pity gave way to compassion. These are my people, I realized. I'm Korean. They're Korean. If not for my grandfather's escape, I would have been born here and would have lived my entire life under juche. My attitude toward the people around me completely changed, and that opened doors to build real relationships with them.

The next day I went for one of my walks through the halls of the hospital. As always, a guard had to come along with me. Instead of feeling sorry for myself, I prayed for the guard.

Lord, give me wisdom in the words I use, I prayed. *Show me how to reveal your truth to him.*

We turned a corner and came to the windows of the courtyard. As always, the dog jumped up on the window, his tail wagging. He acted as if he'd been waiting all day for me to come by.

"Hello, boy," I said. "How is my friend today?"

The dog answered by running along beside us, jumping on the window, and wagging his tail so hard the entire back end of his body shook. The guard gave me a dismissive look.

"Dogs are very popular in America," I said.

"For protection from all the violence?" the guard said.

"No. As pets. Dogs are treated really well in America."

The guard didn't reply. He didn't seem very interested in talking about dogs, so I changed the subject.

"Do you have a family?" I asked.

The guard scowled at me. "Do not ask such things, 103. It is none of your business."

Okay, God, I need some ideas here. We walked along for a little while, not saying anything. I took a loop around through the halls, eventually ending up back by the courtyard, where the dog was waiting for me. Looking over at his friendly face, I decided this dog was my only friend here. Like me, he was a prisoner, or so it seemed. He didn't get to leave the courtyard, and he was pretty much separated from everyone.

I thought about being separated from my family for a moment. I said, "My family is originally from Yongbyon, about sixty miles from here."

The guard seemed surprised. "Really? I thought you were American."

"I am. My family moved to South Korea during the war. I grew up in Seoul. When I was sixteen, we moved to America."

His curiosity was piqued. "How could you just move like that? The government let you?"

"Of course. We had a visa from America. But people in South Korea travel abroad all the time. We do not have to have permission to travel. Anyone can do it."

Now he was hooked. "How can people afford it?"

"The South Korean economy is forty times larger than North Korea's."

He looked like he didn't believe me.

"Really," I said. "The average South Korean household owns a house or apartment and a couple of cars and sends their kids to college."

"No way!" he said, shocked.

"I'm telling you the truth. My family was just a middle-class family, but we had all those things. The same is true in America. We were not rich, but I went both to college and graduate school. I have a master's degree. I owned my own home before I moved to China. My son is in college now."

I could see the wheels spinning in the guard's head. That was my goal with this conversation. Of course I wanted to find a way to tell him about God, but we were a long way from that conversation. All his life he had been taught that juche, self-reliance, was all he needed, along with faith in the Great Leader, Kim Il Sung. On top of that, everything he had heard in the news, in music, and in movies told him that North Korea is the envy of the world. Before he would ever be open to hearing about the one true God, he needed to learn the truth about his own god. I hoped that by telling him about the world beyond his closed society, he might start to question the only "truth" he'd ever known and be open to more of what I had to say.

Eventually we made it back to my room. "Would you like to come in for some tea?" I asked.

The guard looked around. I could tell he wanted to say yes. Clearly he wanted to talk more about the world beyond North Korea. I had piqued his curiosity.

Instead, he said, "No, not now. Perhaps another time."

"Yes," I said. "I would like that."

Doors were starting to open. *God, give me wisdom and patience,* I prayed.

The next day, the guard seemed more relaxed with me. As we walked along I asked, "Are you married?"

"Yes," the guard said.

"What does your wife do?"

"She works in a store."

"My wife had a traditional Korean dress shop in China," I said. "Do you have any children?"

"A son. He's in junior high. I don't get to see him very much when I'm working. I hate that, because he gets sick a lot," the guard said.

I could tell we had turned a corner. The guard talked with me as if I were a friend, not a prisoner on whom he had to keep an eye.

"What kind of sickness?" I asked.

"Colds, mainly."

"Why don't you try giving him extra doses of vitamin C? I take a couple of thousand milligrams a day back home, and I haven't had a cold in years."

The guard perked up. "I think I will try that. Thanks."

About a week later the same guard was on duty. During our walk he said to me, "My wife bought the vitamin C like you suggested, but my son couldn't get it down."

Now, this might not seem like a substantial conversation, but believe me—it was huge. My relationship with the guard had moved to the point where he trusted me enough to take my advice.

"That can be tough. Did you have him chew the tablets up or swallow them whole?" I asked.

"Chew them."

"Have him swallow them with water. That's the only way to get them down," I said.

"Okay. I'll try that when I get home," he said.

I had numerous other conversations like this with other guards throughout my time in the hospital. Some even accepted my invitation to have tea with me. Later on, I even gave Chinese lessons to a few of them and discussed the Chinese movies that played on TV. I still respected them as guards, and they still called me 103, at least when other people were around, but I could tell God was at work.

A few of the guards started asking me questions about God and why I believed. These were not in-depth discussions—not yet—but they were curious because I was so different from anyone they had ever met. I could tell God was answering my prayers. He was using me.

————————————————————————

EIGHTEEN

A Visit from Home

Praise be to the God and Father of our Lord Jesus Christ, the
Father of compassion and the God of all comfort, who comforts
us in all our troubles, so that we can comfort those in any
trouble with the comfort we ourselves receive from God.

—2 Corinthians 1:3–4

A WEEK AND a half after I had come to peace with staying in North Korea for the foreseeable future, Mr. Lee came to see me.

"Your mother is here in Pyongyang. She will be here to see you soon," he said.

"She's here?" I asked, stunned. The Swedish ambassador had told me in his August visit that my mother was trying to arrange a trip to see me, but I never thought it would actually happen.

"Yes. Our government allowed her to come over to visit you as a good-faith gesture. You see, we are not the terrible people the Western media makes us out to be," he said.

Tears welled up in my eyes. "I can't believe it," I said. "Why didn't you tell me she was coming?"

"I thought about it," Mr. Lee said, "but I knew if I said anything ahead of time, you would not be able to sleep or rest until she got here. I hope that is okay with you. She will be here in a few minutes."

I sat on my bed and waited and waited and waited. A few minutes turned into the longest forty minutes of my life. Then I heard the guard on the other side of the door put the key in the lock and turn it.

The door opened. Standing in front of me was my mother.

I jumped up and rushed over to her. As I wrapped my arms around her, we both broke into tears. She grabbed me as though she never wanted to let me go.

When we finally separated, I noticed a film crew in the room, along with several DPRK officials. *Choson Sinbo* was there again, recording everything. All I wanted to do was talk to my mother and find out how my family was doing, but the North Korean officials had other ideas. We had to do an interview first.

"Mrs. Bae," the reporter asked, "did you see the report we did on your son when he was in the labor camp?"

"Yes," my mother said very matter-of-factly. Like me, she did not want to do an interview.

"Well, what did you think of it? How did you feel about the report?" the woman reporter asked with a big smile.

"I didn't like it at all. It was very painful to watch the video clips and see the condition he was in," my mother said. "It made my heart ache." Her tone of voice conveyed even more displeasure, not only with what had happened before, but also with being subjected to these questions now.

"How do you feel seeing your son now?" the reporter asked, oblivious to my mother's discomfort.

"Obviously, I am glad to see my son. However, my hope and desire was to see him back home rather than here. Now, if it is all the same to you, I don't want to do an interview. I am here to see my son."

The reporter looked at the cameraman and then over to Mr. Lee and the other officials in the room. "That's fine. I think we are done here anyway," the reporter said.

The *Choson Sinbo* team left. The North Korean minder assigned to my mother asked her, "Why did you say those things to the reporter?

Don't you know they are trying to help get your son released? Showing disrespect to them is not good, because whatever they report will have a big impact on your son."

"Her questions brought back sad memories, and I didn't want to do an interview anyway," my mom said.

I pulled Mr. Lee over to the side. "Please," I said, "give us as much time as you can. She came all the way from America to see me."

My mother and I had two hours alone together that day and each of the next two days as well. Even though we were alone, I knew our conversations were being listened to from the other room. There's no such thing as total privacy there.

My mother peppered me with all the mom questions: "Are you okay? How are you holding up emotionally? How is your health? How is your back?" I told her I was fine and that I was being treated well. The hospital staff had brought some tea bags and coffee earlier, so I made some tea for my mom. The hospital hadn't just given me these things out of the goodness of their hearts. The day before my mother arrived, I was told that the hospital was billing €600 a day for my time there. If I was going to have to pay that much, I figured I might as well get as much as I could for my money. Over tea I told my mom I was worried about the bill.

"It's true that several past detainees were also required to settle their bills before leaving," she said. "Some paid a few thousand, but there was one who paid as much as half a million dollars."

That didn't make me feel any better. "How are we supposed to do that?" I asked.

"Please do not worry about it. We'll do a fundraising campaign, and the debt will be paid," she said, trying to reassure me.

"I don't know. Maybe I should volunteer to go back to the labor camp right away."

This upset my mom. "No. Don't say that. If you go back there, you will get worse."

I changed the subject. "How is Lydia holding up?" I asked. I knew our time apart had to be very hard for her. Her first husband had died suddenly from a stroke when he was in his early forties. After having one husband suddenly taken from her, I knew she had to be suffering from my being taken from her so quickly as well. We'd only been married four years when I was arrested.

"She couldn't get out of bed for the first three months," my mother said. "But then she found the strength to get up, and she's been taking care of everyone else since then. In fact, the original plan was for both of us to come to see you, but the State Department really discouraged that, because she's not yet a US citizen. If something happened, they wouldn't be able to help her."

As much as I wanted to see my wife, I was thankful she and my mom had changed their plans. I could not live with myself if something happened to Lydia while she was trying to come see me.

The minder who was assigned to my mom then came in and told us that it was time for my mother to go. "Do not worry," he said. "She is coming back tomorrow."

The next day my mother returned with a large bag. "I brought something for you," she said. The next few minutes felt like Christmas morning. She pulled out a box of Hawaiian chocolates with macadamia nuts, some Kit Kat bars, beef jerky, mixed nuts, and protein bars. I couldn't believe my eyes. I had been craving each of these things in exactly the order in which she pulled them out of her bag, but I had never mentioned the cravings in any of my letters. I thought, *Wow, Lord! You really have been listening to the desires of my heart!* She had brought all these treats from the United States. She also went shopping for me in Pyongyang and bought me some noodle soup, soda, and other treats.

In addition my mom gave me several bottles of vitamins, some prediabetes packets, and omega-3, along with some medications and a stack of new books. Two were travel books written by a famous South Korean author, Han Bi Ya. One of the books followed her through the Middle East and parts of Africa, while the other detailed her journeys from Alaska to South America. Those two books allowed me to escape my circumstances in North Korea. I felt like a character in her stories as I traveled with her. I must have read both books at least seven times over the next year.

I think my mother and I talked nonstop for the two hours they gave us on the second day. We had so little time, especially considering how far she had traveled. During the second day she told me she had come over on a one-way ticket. "The round-trip ticket was too expensive," she said.

I nearly lost it. "How are you going to get home?" I asked.

My mom wasn't too worried about it. "Oh, I think I will take a train to Dandong, then fly home from there. That way I can see Lydia as well."

Wow! If I pulled something like that, you would go crazy, I thought, but I didn't say anything. I tried to talk her into doing some sightseeing while she was in Pyongyang—not that I cared about her seeing the sights. I wanted her to meet the people in the city.

"I'm not here to see the sights. I am here to see you," she said.

Even so, she had a lot of extra time and ended up going to a couple of museums. The Swedish ambassador took her out for a steak dinner that night and also treated the government minder and translator from the Swedish embassy. I don't think those two guys had ever had such a meal.

When my mother arrived for her last visit, she brought some noodle soup from a famous restaurant called Okryugwan. Just as mothers do, she didn't just bring enough for the two of us; she also treated the hospital staff and the guards who let her in and out of my room. That made a big impression on them. Rather than act upset and angry with them for what had happened to me, she treated them with kindness. Her actions tore down walls for me to talk to them after she left.

During our last visit, my mom whispered to me that the person named Jane who had been sending me letters along with *New York Times* articles was actually Euna Lee. Euna felt compassion toward me because of her experience in North Korea. She had also started a "Letters for Kenneth" e-mail campaign. Knowing the restrictions the DPRK had on me, she edited all the letters from my supporters and sent them to my mom, who forwarded them to the State Department for me. Euna used an alias just in case the North Korean government recognized her name and refused to give her letters to me.

I was so thankful for her heart and compassion for me. I had already written her a thank-you note without knowing who she really was. In the letter I told "Jane" that I would love to meet her and take her family out for a meal when I got home.

My mother was supposed to be able to stay for only two hours, just as on the previous two days. When the second hour was up, I asked the government minder to please give us more time. He looked over at my mother's pleading eyes and could not say no.

An hour later the minder brought the nurse into the room and started dropping hints that time was up. The nurse couldn't quite bring herself to say the words, so I said them for her.

"Mom, we have to say good-bye."

"No, Kenneth, we need more time," she said.

I looked over at the nurse. "That's all the time we have. I have to do physical therapy now."

"I will ask if I can come see you one more time before I get on the train for Dandong," she said, hopeful.

"You can ask, but they are not going to let you. I'm fine. I will be okay. If I am going to be in North Korea, this is probably the best place for me to be. Don't worry about me. Just keep working on my release," I said. She hesitated. "It's okay, Mom. We will get through this, and then I will have a story to tell for the rest of my life."

My mother had no choice. She gave me a very long good-bye hug. As she was leaving, she looked back at me with an expression I will never forget. Her eyes told me she thought she was never going to see me again. The reality of my situation really hit her right then. Obviously she knew I had been arrested, charged, and convicted. But now, for the first time, she truly understood what it meant that I was a prisoner in North Korea. She had encouraged me to have the faith of Daniel's friends; now she had to do the same.

After my mother left, I did not feel depressed or lonely. Instead, I thanked God for her visit. I knew that finally my family would really know how I was doing. My mom could alleviate a lot of their worries.

We didn't need more worry. Worry wasn't going to change my situation. Only God could do that.

———————————————————

NINETEEN

More Disappointment

Rejoice in the Lord always. I will say it again: Rejoice! Let your gentleness be evident to all. The Lord is near.
—Philippians 4:4–5

MY ONE-YEAR ANNIVERSARY in custody came and went with little fanfare. I got up, read for a while, and then went for a walk through the halls with one of the guards. I got to see my only real friend, the dog, who always made me smile.

At three o'clock in the afternoon, the television came on. The one channel broadcasting that day showed the same propaganda that it showed every day. I tried to ignore it. I read my Bible for a while and then one of the travel books my mother had brought me. Even though I was still in Pyongyang, still a prisoner, the book let me escape to South America for a little while.

The day was pretty much like every other day. When I went to bed that night, I prayed for strength to continue serving God faithfully as a missionary through all the unknown number of days that lay in front of me.

A few days later, a slight man in his late thirties came to see me. "I am the new prosecutor assigned to your case, Mr. Bae. I will check on you every week to see if you need anything. I will also keep you abreast of what is going on with your case." When he spoke, I saw his canine teeth protruded out like a vampire's.

"It is good to meet you," I said. I wanted to start off on a good foot with this man. Thus far most of my experiences with the officials assigned to my case had been overwhelmingly negative. From Mr. Park in Rason, to the chief prosecutor and Mr. Min in Pyongyang, these men vacillated between being unsympathetic and outright hostile toward me. Only Mr. Lee seemed to care about me. Now it looked as if he had been replaced.

"Thank you," he said. "How are you doing today? Do you need anything?"

"I am doing okay," I said.

"Good. Good. Now, as far as your case is concerned, nothing new is going on. Nor do I expect there ever will be." He looked down at the papers in front of him. "It says here that you are forty-six. You and I will spend a lot of time together in the coming years, because you will be here until you are sixty, at least." He did not announce this in a sinister way. Rather, he spoke very matter-of-factly.

"Okay," I said. I looked closely at him to try to tell if he was simply trying to get a reaction from me or if he sincerely believed I was going to serve my entire sentence. Not even the chief prosecutor had ever indicated I would be here for the full fifteen years. During his last visit he had told me the DPRK government would probably let me off for good behavior after seven or eight years.

"Yes, you and I will celebrate your sixtieth birthday here together," he said as he got up to leave. "I will see you next week."

The next week the new prosecutor told me the exact same thing, and the next week and the next and the next. Some weeks he added things like, "Your family has forgotten you. Your government has forgotten you. No one remembers you are even here." He never brought good news, always bad.

I soon started calling the new prosecutor Mr. Disappointment, although I never called him this to his face. To me it seemed his only job was to throw a bucket of cold water on any hopes of release to which I might cling.

Thankfully, Mr. Disappointment's visits often brought new mail for me. In addition to the usual letters from my family, I started receiving letters from strangers who wrote to me as a result of the letter-writing campaigns Euna Lee and others had organized. Mr. Disappointment would tell me everyone had forgotten all about me, but then I would open a new letter and read:

Dear Ken,

Just wanted to let you know that I am praying for you every day. Praying that the Lord may be providing for your emotional, spiritual, and physical needs—in a way that transcends all earthly understanding. *We haven't forgotten about you, brother.*

Much love,

Russ

Hundreds of people like Russ, all telling me how I was not forgotten, wrote to me during my imprisonment. I needed those letters. No matter how strong your faith, and no matter how determined you might be to do God's will whatever the cost, the voice of a Mr. Disappointment can wear you down. Russ and all the people like him carried me through the tough times.

The tough times came on a regular basis. November flew by. When December came, I realized I was going to miss another Christmas with my family. Even though I had made peace with the fact that God had called me to be a missionary in chains for the foreseeable future, it wasn't any easier not to see my wife and children and other family over the holidays.

On December 29, 2013, I was allowed to call my family again. On this call I spoke with my son, Jonathan, for the first time since my arrest. I felt so guilty being away from him for so long.

"This all needed to happen like this right now," I told him, "but don't give up. Keep fighting for me to come home. We are in this together."

Jonathan fought back tears. "I know, Dad. I will not give up. I cannot wait to see you."

"Remind the government that it would be really good if they could get me home before the United States and South Korea hold joint military exercises again in March. When that happened this past March, it seemed that North Korea got mad, and nothing happened on my case for a while."

"We'll do our best," Jonathan said.

"I know you will," I said.

We talked a little about all he had done so far. My son was behind the Change.org petition drive to bring me home. He'd also written the president, the secretary of state, and many other officials, urging them to take action. His efforts, along with the tireless work of my sister and the rest of my family, were beginning to produce results in raising awareness on a grassroots level, although they struggled to gain attention nationally.

And then Dennis Rodman happened.

Basketball Hall of Famer Dennis Rodman brought a team of former professional basketball players to North Korea less than a week after I spoke on the phone with my son. Rodman calls Kim Jong Un his friend, which isn't surprising if you know anything about Dennis Rodman. He has never followed what one might call a traditional path.

This wasn't Rodman's first trip to North Korea while I was imprisoned. He had come alone in early September 2013. When he returned to the United States, reporters asked if he had talked with Kim Jong Un about me. He shouted back, "That's not my job to ask about Kenneth Bae. Ask Obama about that. Ask Hillary Clinton."[1]

On this trip, in early January 2014, Rodman brought with him ten guys who had all played in the NBA. North Korea ate it up. Rodman even sang "Happy Birthday" to Kim Jong Un. I watched it on television in my hospital room. The whole time I felt as if I were watching a scene from *The Twilight Zone*.

During his time in Pyongyang, Rodman and his team did a live interview with Chris Cuomo of CNN. I, obviously, did not get to see the interview, although I did watch the basketball game on television four times that week. I had no choice. It was the only thing on. The North Korean media was very excited about Rodman's "basketball diplomacy" and how he showed such respect to Kim Jong Un. However, Rodman's CNN interview was not broadcast in the DPRK.

In the interview, Cuomo asked Rodman if he planned to speak to Kim about me. Clearly agitated by the question, Rodman replied, "Do you understand what he did in this country? No, no, no, you tell me, you tell me. Why is he held captive here in this country, why?"[2] Later Rodman apologized and said he was drunk when he did the interview.[3] But to everyone watching the interview live, it was clear that Rodman was saying I deserved to be in prison for what I had done. Clearly, he wasn't going to try to talk his buddy into letting me go.

After Rodman's rant on CNN, I became a very hot topic of discussion on the national news networks. Anderson Cooper had my sister back on for an interview. She said, "[Dennis Rodman] was in a position to do some good and to help advocate for Kenneth. He refused to do so but then instead he has chosen to hurl these outrageous accusations against Kenneth." She continued, "He clearly doesn't know anything about Kenneth, about his case, and we were appalled by that."[4]

Apparently, my sister's outrage at Rodman's rant fueled a media frenzy like none my family had seen in the fourteen months of my detainment. My case became high drama played out on live television. More people spoke up for me. In an interview, Bill Richardson again called for my release, as did Vice President Biden. During the National Prayer Breakfast on February 6, 2014, President Obama made a very bold statement. He called me a good man who deserved to be set free.[5] Rev. Jesse Jackson became even more outspoken about my situation. He wrote eleven letters to the North Korean government on my behalf, met with a North Korean delegation at the United Nations, and even volunteered to come to Pyongyang to bring me home.

I later learned that in the wake of the media storm created by Dennis Rodman, my son, my mom, and my sister traveled to New York City for media interviews. They also went to Washington, DC, where they visited with congressmen, senators, and even with Secretary of State Kerry to plead for help from the US government. Congressman Charles Rangel of New York and Congressman Rick Larsen of Washington invited my sister and my mom to attend President Obama's State of the Union address. Thanks to Dennis Rodman's drunken outburst and my sister's defense of me, my case had now catapulted to a new level of national consciousness and outrage.

I didn't know any of this was going on until Mr. Disappointment came storming into my room one afternoon, very upset.

"Do you know what the Western media is saying about you?" he asked. He waved a pile of papers at me. "Just look at this. Look!"

I glanced through the stack of papers. They were printouts of stories about Dennis Rodman's comments and the backlash against him. All the stories said the same thing: North Korea was holding an innocent man who deserved to be set free.

"What are you going to do about this?" Mr. Disappointment demanded.

"What do you mean? What can I possibly do?" I asked.

"You must tell them you are not an innocent man. You are guilty. You admitted it yourself. Maybe we should have you call your family again and set the record straight. Or maybe you can meet with the Swedes and protest this whole thing."

I understood why Mr. Disappointment was so angry. In his eyes, and in the eyes of everyone with whom I had contact in North Korea, I was guilty of a serious crime. On top of that, the message of the gospel of Jesus Christ was a dangerous message that could turn the entire country away from their faith in Kim Il Sung and Kim Jong Il. All throughout the country, large photographs of them adorned houses and public squares. One of my nurses even had to spend a night outside guarding these mosaic portraits against possible vandals. Army officers and loyal party members wore photos of the two on their breasts, next to their hearts. For me to suggest that Jesus, not Kim Il Sung, is Lord was anything but an innocent act in their eyes.

"Why don't you let me hold a press conference?" I suggested. "I will admit that I am guilty of the crimes with which I have been charged, and I will apologize again to North Korea."

"Let me think about that," Mr. Disappointment replied.

"This could be an out for everyone," I said. "I will admit to the world what I have done, and everyone will see that the DPRK is the victim here. Then there will be no reason for you to keep me in custody."

I thought he might go for this. Several times over the previous few weeks, he had dropped hints that they were ready to be rid of me.

The next day Mr. Disappointment returned. "All right, we're going to do what you suggested. In three days you will hold a press conference and admit your guilt. And we want you to address all the people that say you are being held for no reason. Tell them to stop. The vice president and your sister are saying this. You make them stop." Then he added, almost as an aside, "But do not say anything about Dennis Rodman. You leave him out of this."

Just to make sure I said the right thing, Mr. Disappointment then handed me a piece of paper. "Write down your speech and the possible questions and answers from the reporters. You are to practice this speech, but it has to be in your own words. It cannot sound rehearsed."

I felt as though I were back in Rason. "Don't worry," I said. "I am a professional. I speak for a living."

I started practicing that day. Mr. Disappointment did not like what he heard. "You sound like you are reading a script," he complained.

We kept at it all that day and the next. He asked me questions I was supposed to answer. We went over and over my statement. Throughout the rehearsal I understood that if I held this press conference, the North Koreans were going to let me go. That was the deal I thought we had made.

The news conference was scheduled for three o'clock Monday afternoon. In the morning they shaved my head. Then they wanted me to put on my prison uniform. "I left it at the labor camp," I said. Someone went over to get it for me.

Once I looked presentable, they marched me into a conference room on one of the upper floors of the hospital. It was filled with twenty or thirty reporters from news agencies around the world. There were Chinese reporters and Russians, along with reporters from the AP and other major news outlets.

I made my statement professing my guilt and then added, "I believe that my problem can be solved by close cooperation and agreement between the American government and the government of this country." I also said that statements from people like Vice President Biden saying I was being held without reason were only making matters worse.

I knew these statements placed me completely at the mercy of the North Korean government. At the time I believed that anyone watching the news conference would say, "Oh well, he's guilty. He's getting what he deserves." That's basically what Dennis Rodman had said, a statement for which he later apologized. But I knew my saying this would appease the DPRK officials. Now, when they let me go, they would appear to be the humanitarians they believed themselves to be.

Once the press conference ended, Mr. Disappointment escorted me back to my hospital room. He said to me, "Pack your things. You are going back to the labor camp now."

"What?" I said, shocked. This wasn't the deal I thought we had. "I made these statements for you. Why are you punishing me? I thought you would reciprocate and do something for me now, like letting me go home."

"It's better this way. For you to be released you must first go back to the prison."

I didn't say anything in response. I couldn't. I felt like I had made the biggest mistake of my life. I had gone on worldwide television and admitted I deserved what I was getting, and now they were shipping me back to the labor camp to serve out my sentence. I felt as if, instead of letting me go, they were saying to the world, "See, we told you he is guilty. Now we're going to give him what he deserves, and no one can argue with us."

Why would the United States ever send anyone over to negotiate my release now? I am never going to get to go home after this, I thought as I packed my things. I had admitted to antigovernment activities that threatened the whole regime even though all I had done was pray and bring others into the country to pray. For the DPRK, that was a violent act. Anywhere else my actions would be a humanitarian gesture.

You blew it, Ken, I thought over and over.

I packed my things and left the hospital. On the way out I waved good-bye to my one and only friend, the dog.

Mr. Disappointment led me to a waiting minivan in the parking lot, where once again I sat in the middle of the backseat, my head between my knees, while I was driven to an undisclosed location. I wasn't sure where they would take me now. When the doors opened, I thought I might find myself in a regular prison.

After a twenty-minute ride the van came to a stop. I was back at the same labor camp where I had served my first three months.

The guards were all surprised to see me. More than one said things like, "We never thought you would be back here, 103."

I gave them a little smile and replied, "Neither did I."

Unlike my first trip inside the walls, I did not receive an orientation lecture. Instead, I went back to my old room, room 3.

The warden came to see me. "It's a good thing you are here," he said. "You are going to have to work to pay off your hospital bill." I had made about $0.25 a month for my hard labor. The hospital had charged me €600 a day for five months. By the time I was sent back to the labor camp, my bill had come to more than €101,000, or about $120,000.

I would have to work forty thousand years of hard labor just to pay off my bill.

I didn't say anything about that. I just smiled and said, "It is nice to be someplace familiar."

Finally, Mr. Disappointment, the warden, and the guards left me alone in my cell. I looked around and let out a long sigh. Four months earlier I had told God that I was giving up my right to go home. I had embraced his will and told him that I would stay here as long as he wanted. Yet I had never thought his will would lead me back to the labor camp, back to serving out my sentence with no end in sight.

I sat on my bed, my mind spinning as I tried to make sense of it all. Finally I prayed, *All right, Lord. This is really hard for me, but I want your will, not mine. Use me in this place, Father. Use me.*

————————————————————————————

TWENTY

MISSIONARY IN CHAINS

If you suffer as a Christian, do not be ashamed, but praise God that you bear that name.

—1 PETER 4:16

THE WARDEN HAD been as shocked as I was when I climbed out of the minivan and walked in the front gate. He had even told me, "We didn't know you were coming right away." He had scrambled around to find some heavy clothing for me to wear and to find something for me to do.

However, by the next morning he had recovered. At eight o'clock sharp the warden sent me a guard, who then led me outside. My whole body tensed up the moment I walked out the door. The temperature hovered around fifteen degrees. I had no idea where he was taking me or what the warden had in store for me to do. I just knew it was cold.

The last time I was here, I baked in the sun while pulling weeds from my soybean field. Now I thought I might freeze to death if I stayed outside very long.

The guard led me around a corner, and I saw a huge pile of ash. "This is your new assignment, 103. This pile is the ash left over from the coal we use to keep the prison warm."

I nodded. "What do you want me to do with it? Do you want me to haul it away somewhere?"

"No. In juche we utilize everything we have. This ash fertilizes our fields. However, as you can see, it is all clumped together." He motioned toward a pickax lying on the ground. "Use that pickax over there to break the clumps into powder."

"Do you have a mask I can wear to protect my lungs from the dust?" I asked.

The guard shook his head. "No, nothing like that. You don't need a mask. It's a simple job. Even you can do this without messing it up, 103."

I smiled. "Yes, you're probably right. Even a missionary can figure out how to use this," I said as I grabbed the pickax.

I lifted the ax up over my head and let it fall down on a stack of ash clumps. They easily broke up into smaller clumps as dust sprayed up and over me. I then turned the ax on its head and used the flat part to grind the ashes into the consistency of sand.

I soon found myself enveloped in a dust cloud. The dust was so heavy I could hardly see through my glasses. My nose itched. I had to stop from time to time because I sneezed so hard. But I kept after it, breaking up clumps of coal ash to turn them into fertilizer.

Two guards sat on the ground not far from me, trying to stay out of the dust cloud as best they could. A third guard stayed inside the building, where it was warm. All the guards were very relaxed. One appeared to doze off at one point. By this point I knew most of these guys really well. Some of the guards from the camp were also my guards in the hospital. Over the previous four months I had had many conversations with each of them, talking about everything from their families to the cost of living in Pyongyang to where one of them got the money for his cigarette habit.

I was hacking away at the ash clumps when one of the guards said, "So you never got any special training?"

"Like what?" I said.

"You know, lethal training. That's what the CIA does, right?" Even after all this time, deep down they still suspected I was part of the CIA.

"Oh, sure," I said, kidding.

Another said, "Are you one of those killing machine guys?"

"Yes, I am," I said. "I can take you down in no time. I just don't do it because I enjoy breaking up this ash so much."

That line got a good laugh.

"You know," I said, "if I am CIA, then that means there's a satellite watching me right now. You never know. My commander might send a team of commandos in to rescue me at any moment." I grinned after saying this.

The two guards glanced at each other and then looked up. The first said, "Come on, 103. Really?"

"No. I'm just a missionary. I tell people about God. The only thing I know about the CIA is what I see in the movies, and I know that's not accurate."

One of the guards got up, looked back up at the sky, and announced, "I'm going to go in to warm up for a few minutes. You got this?" he asked the other guard.

"Yeah. Go ahead," the other said.

I now found myself one-on-one with a guard. He waited a couple of minutes before saying, "You mentioned God. I've never really understood the appeal of believing in God. I know people are born knowing they have to lean on something. But to say that that something is God, that doesn't make a lot of sense. You can't see God. I mean, I can see the Supreme Leader. That's who I depend on."

"What does he do for you?" I asked.

"He provides for me. Food, housing, that sort of thing. We have free medical care here. Free education. And jobs. Sometimes I even work for free," he said with a laugh. Like everyone else, the guards had to do the extra work of clearing the highway of snow that I saw people doing when I traveled from Rason to Pyongyang. No one received any kind of pay for that work. It was everyone's privilege, a way of working together for the common good. That was supposed to be payment enough.

"I heard housing is hard to come by now," I said.

"Yeah, that's true. The government doesn't really give that away anymore. An apartment here in Pyongyang is really expensive. Most people can't afford it. It is so expensive because of the 'military first' policy. So much has to go to protect us from America that there's not a lot left over. However, because I am a military officer, the government provides me a place to live." For the guard to talk so openly meant he was very comfortable with me.

"I know a lot about the problem expensive housing can be," I said. Then I told him the story of how God provided a place for my YWAM team in Dalian, and later in Dandong. "One time, God provided us with about $75,000, which is nearly 615 million North Korean *won*," I said.

The guard's jaw dropped; his eyes grew wide. "Your God did that?"

"Yes," I said. "When God asks someone to do something for him, he provides what that person needs to do it. Money, people, materials—it doesn't matter. God is bigger than any of it."

"It couldn't be God. It had to be a coincidence," the guard said.

"How could it be a coincidence? My team and I prayed for specific amounts of money, and then we received the exact amount we asked God for from someone we had never even met. We didn't ask people for the money, only God. If it were a coincidence, my life is one big coincidence. God has always provided for me. He protects me. He takes care of me like a loving father cares for his children," I said.

"If he cares so much about you, why are you still in prison and not able to go home?" the guard asked. He looked as though he had just played his trump card.

"He has me in here because he cares for you and for all of North Korea. He wants you to know who he is and how much he loves you," I said.

My answer seemed to shake him. "Get back to work," he said.

I had conversations like this one throughout my second stay in the labor camp. Some of the guards weren't with me in the hospital, so I didn't have the advantage of having already built a relationship with them. That didn't matter. I started the conversation by asking them questions about themselves, questions like, "If Korea is unified, what city do you want to visit first?" or something as basic as, "Do you like music?" or "What is your favorite Korean dish?"

Some of the guards refused to talk to me. Most, however, warmed up to me. It made the time pass faster for both of us.

᪥

After my first day of work, I went back to my room, covered with ash from head to toe. My whole body ached. Thankfully, hot water was available. I took a shower using a bucket to dump water over my head.

After my shower I dropped down in my chair, wishing ten o'clock would come soon so that I could go to bed. My back ached. My hands, which had been numb during my first time in the labor camp, were numb again. Worse yet, I started coughing and could hardly stop. And I kept sneezing. Every time I sneezed or blew my nose, thick black stuff came out.

Even so, the next morning I was back outside, breaking up clumps of ash and talking with the guards. I joked around with them a lot.

One asked me once, "Why are you so happy? You're always joking and singing. This isn't supposed to be a pleasant experience."

"What are you talking about?" I replied. "I've got free room and board here. Usually I have to raise support for my missionary work, but not now. I even wanted to be a missionary in North Korea. Now I get to, and I get to be with you guys. I want to be here with you. Why shouldn't I be happy?"

That answer made them think I was crazy.

Another day a guard asked, "How can you believe in God when you can't see him?"

"When you turn on a light, you can't see the electricity, but you know it is there," I said. "It's the same with God. Think about the wind. You can't see the wind, but you know it is there. I can't see God, but I know he is here."

"That's different," the guard replied.

"No, it's not. I not only know God is here, but he communicates with me through the Bible. He also speaks to me through his Spirit."

"What?" the guard said. "What planet are you from?"

"I'm serious. God spoke to me right after high school and told me he wanted me to be a missionary to China. That's how I ended up in Dandong. Later he told me he wanted me to be a bridge from North Korea to the world. That's why I started coming into the DPRK. I brought people here to see the land, meet the people, and pray for you. God has even spoken to me while I have been in prison. In the very beginning he told me that he was going to take care of me and I would not be harmed. He has done exactly that."

The guard really took this in. I could tell he was thinking about what I said. Later on, several of the guards asked me at different times if God had said anything to me lately. That told me the guards discussed among themselves my conversations with them. They weren't mocking me; they seriously wanted to know if God had spoken to me recently.

I also had a lot of conversations with the guards about their families. I found that most marriage problems are universal. Eventually the guards started coming to me for advice. In front of their superiors they always called me 103, but when we were alone, just the two of us, they said, "Pastor, can you help me with a problem?"

They asked a lot of questions about my wife. "How do you know she will still be there when you get out?" more than one asked. That gave me an opportunity to talk about the most important parts of marriage, like trust and love and having God at the center of your relationship. Some days I found I was doing as much marriage counseling as I was breaking up ash clumps.

It wasn't just the guards with whom I had in-depth conversations. About once a week the warden came by. Other times the deputy warden came to see me. Both asked if I had heard anything from home and if I had any indication of when I might be released. I also had many conversations with them about politics and the tension between North Korea and America.

Three weeks after I arrived back in the labor camp, the new Swedish deputy ambassador, Cecilia Anderberg (who replaced John Svensson), came to inform me that special ambassador Robert King was on his way to North Korea to negotiate my release.

"Rev. Jesse Jackson wanted to come, but the Obama administration sent Ambassador King instead. He will arrive on Monday." She gave me this news on a Friday.

I cannot describe the excitement and relief I felt when she told me this. I wanted to jump up and down and celebrate. However, I kept it together and thanked her.

"This is great news," I told her. "I wish he were coming today, but I think I can hold on one more weekend."

I didn't say it, but I wasn't sure I could last much beyond the weekend. Only three weeks had passed since my news conference, but it seemed like more. My food rations were now much smaller than they had been my first time in the labor camp. Back then I had bread occasionally, and vegetables, and even meat and eggs. Not this time. At first I thought that withholding food must be some kind of punishment. After a couple of weeks I realized no one in the camp had much to eat, not me or the guards or any of the staff. As a result, weight fell off of me. My other ailments, including my bad back and numb hands, were also back. That made the news that someone was coming for me even sweeter.

I woke up excited on Monday morning. The guards and other officials treated the day just like any other. I went back to the ash pile. I had already told the guards that I might not be there much longer. I even sang a good-bye song to them.

One of the guards said, "Don't sing such a sad song. You are making me sad. You should stay longer so we can have more conversations."

I wanted to minister to these guys, but I was ready to go home. Throughout the day, I kept waiting for the warden to come tell me to drop the ax and go pack my things. But he never came. I watched for Ambassador King to walk through the prison gate, but he never arrived. The day passed like every other day. No one came.

No one came the next day. Or the next. Or the next. Every day that week I woke up thinking it was going to be my last day in the camp, and every day I went to bed disappointed.

Finally, on Saturday, Mr. Disappointment arrived for his weekly visit. He didn't waste any time before crushing my hopes once and for all.

"Your ambassador's trip was cancelled. We withdrew his invitation. No one is coming for you. No one cares about you. No one even remembers you are here. You need to stop hoping for an early release and understand you and I will celebrate your sixtieth birthday here together."

I did my best not to react to his news, but it was difficult. Honestly, I was not surprised. Since a week had passed since Ambassador King was supposed to arrive, I already knew he wasn't coming. Mr. Disappointment only confirmed my fears. Twice now Pyongyang had offered to have Ambassador King come to negotiate my release only to pull the invitation at the last minute. I decided that the next time I was told people were on their way to take me home, I would not believe it until I actually saw them with my own eyes and heard them say, "I'm taking you out of here now."

The Monday after I thought I was going home, I received a new assignment. The guards led me to the middle of the prison yard. Some pipe lay off to the side.

"We need to lay a new sewage line. You are going to dig the trench," I was told.

Now I had finally arrived. I was a ditch digger.

I found digging a trench through frozen ground to be the most difficult assignment yet. The pickax bounced off the hard dirt, barely even making a dent. For eight hours I slammed the pointed end of the ax into the ground and then spun it around and tried to move some dirt with the flat end. Even in the bitter cold, sweat poured off me. My hands became numb, and my back was killing me. But I kept on digging. I had no choice.

The next morning I woke up and discovered it was snowing. I was as happy as a little boy on a snow day. I couldn't dig the trench in the snow.

But that didn't mean I got off from work; instead the guards had me shovel snow. However, there was far too much for one person to handle. I actually worked side by side with the guards, all of us shoveling away. I had a lot of really good conversations with the guards while shoveling. On other snow days I went back to pounding clumps of coal ash. That beat ditch digging.

My health got worse quickly. My cough would not go away, and my weight kept dropping. All the weight I had put back on during my time in the hospital was now gone. To make matters worse, I had developed a terrible toothache. The pain had first flared up while I was in the hospital. The dentist there had suggested doing oral surgery to remove it. The thought of having oral surgery in North Korea didn't exactly thrill me, so I had decided to wait. The dentist had given me an antibiotic, which made the pain go away for a while.

Unfortunately, the pain had come back even stronger not long after I returned to the labor camp. I went to see my old friend the camp doctor, the same one who had told me that hard work would heal whatever was wrong with me. The fact that I willingly went to see him tells you how much my tooth hurt. The pain was some of the worst I had experienced in my life.

I told the doctor, "When this happened in the hospital, they gave me an antibiotic, and it cleared it up."

"No antibiotics," he snapped back. "Too many antibiotics are bad for you."

"I know," I said, "but I cannot eat and I cannot sleep and I cannot work. The pain is more than I can take."

"I'll give you some aspirin. That should take care of it," he said. "Place the aspirin underneath your gum next to the tooth and hold it there, and you will feel much better."

I am not a doctor, but I knew this was a terrible plan. "I need an antibiotic plus the aspirin," I argued.

That set him off. "I am the doctor, not you! I have been to medical school. Have you? Who are you? You don't know anything."

We had this same conversation for ten straight days. Finally, I wore him down. "Tell you what," he said. "I will take care of your pain with acupuncture."

The fact that I let him do this tells you how much pain I was in. From the outside he inserted a giant needle through my cheek and into my gum. Believe it or not, the pain stopped for a couple of days. That side of my face just went numb. But the pain came back, which started the whole argument over again.

Later on one of the guards suggested I place vitamin C tablets under the gum next to the tooth. He told me he had done this for a toothache, and it helped. Desperate, I tried it, and it worked.

When I next went to see the doctor, he said to me, "See, I told you. The aspirin works."

Eventually, I quit going to see the doctor. I already knew his answers to all my complaints: "Of course your back hurts. This is a labor camp . . . Work hard and your hands will get better . . . Yes, you've lost weight. You look much better now."

Mr. Disappointment came to see me again. I continually interrupted his "No one remembers you; no one cares for you" speech with coughing fits.

"Have you seen the doctor about that?" he asked.

I laughed. "No. His prescription for everything is more work."

"I will check into it," he said.

One week later I was transported from the camp to the hospital. An X-ray found a spot on my lung. I had also lost thirty-five pounds in my two and a half months back at the labor camp. I was admitted back into the hospital, where I returned to my familiar room down at the end of the hall. I had no illusions about going home this time. I just hoped they would let me stay there for a while. I dared not dream any bigger.

TWENTY-ONE

Is That What Is Going to Happen to Me?

Be strong and take heart,
all you who hope in the LORD.

—Psalm 31:24

AFTER I RETURNED to the hospital on March 27, 2014, the care I received was noticeably different from my first stay, especially when it came to my meals. Before I had been served fruit with many of my meals. I had also enjoyed extras, such as coffee and tea, which I kept in my room and could drink whenever I wanted. I had asked for and gotten treats, such as cookies and even ice cream. Part of the reason, I was certain, was they wanted to get my weight back up to something close to normal in anticipation of sending me home. They didn't want me to look malnourished when I stepped off the plane in front of the world media for the first time.

The extras were gone when I returned to the hospital. No fruit. No coffee. No ice cream. No small treats. The meals were plain, small, and predictable. They rotated a handful of meager menu options. On top of that, no one seemed to want to bring my meals to me. As a prisoner in a locked room, I could not get the meals myself. During my first visit, the nurse on duty had brought a tray in to me. Now I saw her outside my door, arguing with the guard and trying to get him to carry it in. Eventually the guard came in with the food, clearly unhappy.

"This isn't my job," he grumbled as he dropped the tray just inside my door. Looking over at me he said, "Come get your food. You're a prisoner. I'm not going to bring it all the way across the room to you."

After several days I finally asked the guard what was going on. "Why is everything so different this time?"

"You haven't paid your bill from the first time you were in here. You owe the hospital a lot of money. They can't afford to do much for you until it is paid," he said.

Mr. Disappointment had told me that I owed €101,000 from my first hospital stay. He wanted me to ask the Swedish ambassador to ask the United States government to pay my bill before they admitted me a second time. I had already signed a promissory note pledging upon my release to repay the US government for any expenses I incurred, including my hotel bill from Rason and all my medical bills. I guess they thought the United States would just hand over money to them after that. When they didn't, the North Koreans expected me to pay it. With the exchange rate at that time, the total had already come to around $130,000.

"I don't have access to that kind of money," I said to Mr. Disappointment.

"You better come up with some sort of plan," Mr. Disappointment said. "Health care is free for North Koreans, but you aren't North Korean." The level of care I now received because of my unpaid bill reinforced how true that statement really was.

The only upside to being back in the hospital was I got to see my only friend in North Korea. On my first walk through the halls, I went over and tapped on the glass of the courtyard window. Immediately the dog jumped up. As soon as he saw me, he jumped against the window, barked, and wagged his tail so hard I thought his legs were going to fly off the ground. It was nice to see a friendly face, even if it was the face of a dog I could interact with only through a window.

The dog was the only one glad to see me. Mr. Disappointment kept up his regular visits with me. As if it were possible, he brought even more disappointment than before.

"It is highly unusual nothing has been done to get you home," he said. "It looks like they have forgotten all about you. I don't think you are going anywhere." He always said that. Then he dropped a new bomb: "I don't know if anyone has already told you this, but the time you spend in the hospital does not count toward your fifteen years. Only the time you spend in the labor camp counts toward your sentence," he said.

I did the math in my head. I had been sentenced on April 30, 2013. Since then I had spent five and a half months in the labor camp, and five and a half months and counting in the hospital. At this rate, my sentence looked more like thirty years than fifteen. Now I was really depressed.

However, not long after my return to the hospital, Ms. Cecilia Anderberg, from the Swedish embassy, came back to see me. She brought me some magazines and newspapers that were a few months old already, along with some fresh mail. She also gave me some treats, such as chocolates, cookies, and even Diet Coke. The magazines gave me a glimpse of the world beyond my walls, which helped. The mail revived my soul.

"Stay strong," she told me. "People are working very hard to get you home."

As soon as she left, a guard took away the treats before I could taste even one. Mr. Disappointment told me that it was for my own safety. "We cannot allow food from outside without inspection," he explained.

I never saw the treats again. Someone enjoyed the treats, but it wasn't me.

Spring gave way to summer. Summer 2014 was very hot in North Korea. By the first of July it had climbed to one hundred degrees nearly every day. My room was somewhat air-conditioned, which helped. The hallways were very hot when I went out for my walks.

I felt sorry for my friend the dog. He had a thick, light brown coat of fur. He had to be miserable in this heat. Even so, he was always so glad to see me when I walked past the window. Like me, he was stuck here, a prisoner. He appeared to be nearly as forgotten as I was. When I walked past him, I said to him in my mind, *No one knows how I feel except you. You and me, we're the same here. Prisoners.*

No one even knew his name. I asked the guards and even a couple of the nurses, but no one seemed to know or care. That only made me relate to him more. I didn't have a name either, just a number.

One July morning I walked past the dog's window and tapped on it, but he didn't jump up. I looked around the courtyard, wondering where he might be. He had never failed to greet me until today.

The courtyard looked different. The dog had made a mess of the place. An old Ping-Pong table had sat in one corner, and he had chewed a good-sized chunk off of it. Today the table was gone, and the courtyard was clean. It almost looked as if the dog had never been there. *I wonder where they took him*, I thought.

Then it hit me.

Today was the beginning of a Korean festival known as *Sambok*, which celebrates the hottest season of the year. The first day of *Sambok* is called *Chobok*. Traditionally, Korean families have a feast on this day. When I was growing up in Seoul, we celebrated with a chicken dinner. But that is not the traditional dish among the poor families of North Korea. They cannot afford chicken, so they use a different source of protein.

My heart sank as I went back to my room. All I could think about was the dog, my friend, the only one in all of North Korea who genuinely seemed to care about me.

About an hour after I returned to my room, my door opened. The head nurse brought in my lunch. Instead of the usual semi-Western-style meal I normally ate, she carried in a big, steaming bowl of soup. I glanced down at it. The soup was loaded with meat.

I didn't have to ask, but I did. "Is that . . . ?" I couldn't say it. "Is that . . . the dog that was in the courtyard?"

The nurse smiled and said, "Yes. It is a celebration day. Enjoy."

I nearly threw up. "No, no, no, take it away. I cannot eat it."

The nurse looked at me as though I had lost my mind. In her eyes, how could anyone pass up such a rare treat?

"Are you sure?" she said, not wanting me to miss out.

"Yes, please take it away. Bring me anything but that."

"Okay," she said, confused. "Suit yourself." She carried the soup out of the room, disappointed.

A little while later she returned with some fried chicken and a bowl of broth. Apparently they had cooked the chicken very quickly, because when I cut into it, blood oozed near the bone. I dropped it back on the plate. I decided I wasn't hungry after all.

I walked back to my bed and collapsed on it. All I could think about was my friend. Even though we had never actually touched, I missed him terribly. The two of us were alike. Prisoners. Forgotten.

Is that what is going to happen to me? I wondered. *Are they just toying with me before they chop me up, not literally but metaphorically? Is my time in this prison going to end as horribly as the dog's?*

As I write this more than a year later, my heart remains heavy. I still miss my friend.

The weeks turned into months. Mr. Disappointment grew more and more agitated during his visits, as if it were my fault I was still a prisoner.

Unbeknownst to me, several people had offered to come to North Korea to negotiate my release. These included Rev. Jesse Jackson, Franklin Graham, and Congressman Charles Rangel of New York. That wasn't good enough for the North Koreans. In 2009, when Laura Ling and Euna Lee were in prison, former president Clinton came over. That's what they wanted this time. Twice they had rejected special ambassador

Robert King, and they had refused to talk to former New Mexico governor and UN ambassador Bill Richardson when he had come over.

More than once I brought up Ambassador King and Bill Richardson with Mr. Disappointment. Every time he replied, "Why don't they send someone higher up?" Higher up meant a former president.

"Who would you have them send?" I asked one day. "There are only four former presidents living. Jimmy Carter is nearly ninety and in poor health. He can't come. Clinton's wife is going to run for president in 2016. He can't do anything that will jeopardize her campaign. That leaves George Bush and George W. Bush. I don't think you want either of them." I didn't have to say it, but I knew the North Koreans hated George W. Bush for labeling them as part of the axis of evil after September 11. "So who do you want to come?"

"Well, that wasn't a problem in 2009," Mr. Disappointment replied. After hearing this many times, I finally said, "You want Clinton? Okay, I will write letters saying you want President Clinton to return for me, but I am telling you, it won't work."

I wrote a letter to my sister asking her to request President Clinton come over. I did it only to appease Mr. Disappointment and everyone else who read my letters before they were sent. When the Swedish deputy ambassador came to see me in August 2014, she told me flat out, "The State Department said President Clinton cannot come."

I repeated this news to Mr. Disappointment, who I assume relayed the information up the chain of command. He seemed very disappointed by the news. I think he and everyone else in the DPRK leadership were ready to be rid of me once and for all.

At the end of July 2014, Mr. Disappointment decided I needed to do another interview to increase the pressure on the Obama administration. I suggested we open it to all media again.

"No, that is not a good idea," he said.

"What about just CNN or AP instead of *Choson Sinbo*?" I asked.

He gave my suggestion a lot of thought, then finally consented. But when it came time to do the interview, only *Choson Sinbo* was there. Apparently, the DPRK leadership trusted only their unofficial voice to the outside world.

Right before the interview, Mr. Disappointment said to me, "You are going back to the labor camp as soon as this is over. Make sure you say that."

I was not surprised. After nearly two years in custody, I had come to understand this tactic was all part of their strategy. They made threats, put me in front of a camera, and had me beg the United States to do something. Finally, to show how serious they were, they sent me to the labor camp to carry out my fifteen-year sentence. The message was clear: "If you want your people back, you better get over here and humble yourself before the Supreme Leader."

The morning of my latest *Choson Sinbo* interview, my nails were trimmed and my head shaved. Unlike before, I did not have to write out my statements ahead of time, although Mr. Disappointment asked me what I was going to say.

"Just stick with the main themes," he reminded me. "You need your government to bring you home, so ask for it."

When the interview started, I said to the camera, "I feel left behind by the US government." I repeated the statement in both English and Korean to make my meaning clear. I used the words *left behind* rather than *abandoned* because the latter was too strong of a term. Up until this point I had never said anything negative about either the United States or the DPRK governments. I had always thanked the United States for all they were doing and urged them to keep trying. But this time I knew I needed to use a phrase that would grab a headline back home.

I made a few more statements and then closed with, "I am going back to the labor camp right after this interview."

That caught the reporter off guard. "You mean today?" she asked.

"Yes. As soon as we are through here, I will be escorted back."

The interview ended. I was told to pack. A few minutes later I found myself back in the middle seat of a minivan with covered windows, on my way to the prison camp for the third time.

When I walked back into room 3 in the labor camp on July 29, 2014, the guards seemed genuinely shocked. More than one said, "We've never had anyone come back here a third time."

"You know me," I said. "I just can't stay away."

I had been away for four months. It was spring when I left. Now it was one of the hottest summers anyone could remember, much hotter than the year before. My room was sweltering. However, because we hadn't had much rain, fewer bugs invaded my room through my open window. I was thankful for that.

On Wednesday, July 30, I reported for work. The field had already been planted, so the warden had to find something else for me to do. The guards were working on a new road on one side of the prison compound, so they put me to work on it as well. On one side of the prison yard was a dried stream. In the stream's bed were round rocks about six inches across. My job was to move rocks from the stream to the road, a distance of about 150 yards.

The prison gave me a four-wheel cart to use for my work. I piled rocks into the cart, pushed it across uneven ground to the other side of the yard, dumped them out, and placed them wherever the guards wanted them. By noon the temperature was close to 100, with very high humidity. By midafternoon it had to be at least 105. I stripped off my uniform shirt to stay cool. Unfortunately, the sun baked my back. When it came time for meals, I didn't have much of an appetite. Although I must have drunk at least two gallons of water a day, I never had to take a bathroom break.

In spite of the heat I sang throughout the day. I started singing in the morning as I got ready to go outside. I sang while I worked. And I sang in the evenings during the power outages that occurred nearly every day.

When the electricity went off, I could not read or watch TV, so I sat in the complete darkness of my cell and sang love songs to Jesus. I was so tired I could not even open my eyes, and my body ached, yet I thanked God for letting me endure another day. It was my time with my Savior and Lord.

Singing through the day was nothing new for me. But this time I found myself singing the same song over and over. Sometimes in English, sometimes in Korean, I sang an old hymn by James Black called "Where Jesus Is, 'Tis Heaven." I love the lyrics:

> *Since Christ my soul from sin set free,*
> *This world has been a Heav'n to me;*
> *And 'mid earth's sorrows and its woe,*
> *'Tis Heav'n my Jesus here to know.*

> *O hallelujah, yes, 'tis Heav'n,*
> *'Tis Heav'n to know my sins forgiv'n,*
> *On land or sea, what matters where?*
> *Where Jesus is, 'tis Heaven there.*

> *Once Heaven seemed a far off place,*
> *Till Jesus showed His smiling face;*
> *Now it's begun within my soul,*
> *'Twill last while endless ages roll.*

> *What matters where on earth we dwell?*
> *On mountain top, or in the dell,*
> *In cottage, or a mansion fair,*
> *Where Jesus is, 'tis Heaven there.[1]*

I changed the words to the last verse, however. Instead of "In cottage, or a mansion fair," I sang, "In hospital or in prison."

The guards, I knew, were listening, especially on the dark nights, when sound travels far. The entire camp could hear the singing of an American Christian prisoner. Everyone there knew I was in chains because of my faith in God. When my faith did not waver, even after being sent to the labor camp for an unprecedented third time, they started to ask, "What is it you have that I don't? How can you sing and be joyful at desperate and hopeless hours? Where does your hope come from?"

Not long after I came back to the labor camp, a guard came to me privately and asked, "Pastor, what benefit would I get if I believe in God like you?" I think he knew the answer just from the song he had heard me sing. Then he asked, "What price do I have to pay to believe in God like you? What will it cost me?" I explained how there is no financial cost. However, to believe in Jesus means surrendering all to him.

Then came the final question, the one that I could tell bothered him the most. "If God is real, why are you still here? You have been here longer than any other prisoner."

I answered honestly. I told the guard that it was God's plan for me to be there, and that plan includes him and the other guards. "Without me, how would you hear about God and Jesus, his Son?"

The guard thought for a moment. "That's true. I have never heard any of this before," he said. The guard didn't follow up with another question. Instead, he went back to his post, thinking carefully about our conversation.

It's funny. When all I had wanted to do was go home, my conversations with the guards had never gone very deep. However, once I accepted this place as God's will for my life, and I started praying, *God, use me*, instead of *God, save me*, doors opened.

Don't get me wrong. My third stay in the labor camp was miserable, physically and emotionally. Day upon day of hot, backbreaking work wrecked my body. I woke up every hour at night because my hands were numb and my body ached. My pain was real, and it was intense. But even in the midst of my suffering, God was with me. His presence is why I was able to rejoice in my suffering, and that is what opened up doors to truly share the good news with those around me.

When I took the words of the old hymn seriously and truly believed that "Where Jesus is, 'tis Heaven there," then and only then did the doors swing open for God to really use me to touch people's lives. I had become the missionary I prayed I could be.

TWENTY-TWO

Not Alone

Do not repay evil with evil or insult with insult. On the contrary, repay evil with blessing, because to this you were called so that you may inherit a blessing.

—1 PETER 3:9

CECILIA ANDERBERG, THE Swedish deputy ambassador, came to see me two weeks after my return to the labor camp. As she usually did, she brought me some newspapers, new magazines, and some chocolate. (The chocolate disappeared the moment she left, as it always did.) On this visit she also brought me something better than chocolate: news that two other Americans were in custody in the DPRK and would face trial.

I wanted to ask her what they had done and if they were missionaries like me. If they were, then I thought the North Koreans were in trouble. Two of us made a company; three was a church! But I did not ask, because I knew the DPRK officials listening in on our conversation did not want me to know such things. Even without knowing what the two new American prisoners had done, I knew this was good news for me. With three of us in custody, the odds of a deal being worked out between the North Koreans and the Obama administration increased. Ms. Anderberg also assured me that she was going to try to have me sent back to the hospital, for which I was thankful.

Two weeks later Mr. Disappointment came to see me. "You're going to get your wish to do an interview with the Western media," he said.

"Who is coming?" I asked.

"I don't know," he said. "Maybe the AP, maybe CNN. I don't know. Whoever it is, you must do this one right. Maybe something good will happen if you do."

On September 1, 2014, I reported for work just like any other day. Before my first break the deputy warden came out to get me.

"We're going to give you a haircut before your interview," he said.

I was disappointed. They were going to shave my head again. I had hoped to grow my hair out a little before I was released. He led me back to the barber, but the regular guy who cut my hair wasn't there. Someone else took over. Unfortunately, the new barber wasn't much of a barber. He didn't have the right clippers, and he didn't know what he was doing.

The replacement barber had cut maybe two-thirds of my hair when Mr. Disappointment came in and said, "It's time."

"That's enough, then. Stop the haircut. Let's go," the deputy warden said.

I looked at myself in the mirror. My half-shaved head made me look like some kind of mad scientist. "Can't he finish first?" I asked.

"No," he said. "There's no time."

"Can I at least wash my hair to get all the loose hair off me?" I asked.

"There's no time. You look fine," the deputy warden said.

One of the guards brought some clothes for me to change into. I recognized them as some my mother had sent me. I was happy to get to wear real clothes for a change. However, when I put on the pants, they basically fell off me because I had lost so much weight. In the month that I had been back in the labor camp, I had dropped another fifteen pounds.

"Do you have my belt?" I asked. I had had a nice belt when I had entered North Korea.

The warden said, "Here, you can use mine." He handed me his belt, and I put it on. I had to cinch it up really tight, and even then it felt like my pants might fall off.

Once I changed my clothes, I was transported from the labor camp to a hotel that also had a restaurant in it. Mr. Disappointment and the guards led me to a second-floor private room, just off the restaurant. There I sat and waited with the guards for a solid hour.

"See, I told you I had time to get my hair cut," I said, but no one listened.

All of a sudden, a CNN crew walked into the room. Until I met them I had no idea with whom my interview might be. I later learned that the other two American prisoners were in rooms just down the hall. The CNN crew interviewed each of us, one at a time. One, Jeffrey Fowle, was arrested when he left a Bible behind in an international sailors' club bathroom. I later learned he was released three short weeks after this interview. The other, Matthew Miller, entered the country legally with a tourist visa. However, as soon as he arrived, he tore up his visa and asked for asylum. The North Koreans arrested him as a spy. He went to trial and was sentenced to six years of hard labor. I did not know any of this at the time.

Will Ripley, the CNN reporter, told me at the outset that we had only five minutes. He was very nice and tried to give me as much time as possible to address my family as well as the United States government. I made it clear that I believed the only way my situation would ever be solved was through a special envoy coming over to negotiate my release. I also chose my words very carefully so as not to antagonize the DPRK government. When asked about my conditions and treatment, I said I was being treated humanely.

After the interview I was transported back to the labor camp. The warden immediately came to see me and asked, "What did they ask you?"

I joked with him and said, "The CNN reporter asked if I was being treated humanely or inhumanely. What else can I say but humanely?"

"What do you mean? We haven't violated your human rights," he replied.

"Nothing counts until I leave the country. That's all people in the United States care about. As long as I am here, they see it as inhumane treatment. Sure, I haven't been beaten up, but that doesn't count for much with Americans."

I guess I made him feel a little guilty, because the next day he told me, "We have a new job for you. Instead of moving rocks outside, we have an indoor job for you. You are going to peel corn."

Then he added, "I just want you to know that we are treating you as humanely as possible. You make sure you say that when you get out of here." His last statement told me something was up. The warden expected me to be gone soon.

A buzz came over the prison two weeks after my interview. Guards rushed about, carrying blankets into one of the rooms. When it came time for me to go to work, they gave me a broom and had me sweep room 7. That was on a Saturday. The next day I was told to go to the bedroom part of my room and stay away from my door. They didn't want me to see something, and I had a pretty good idea what it was. My lunch came, but they pushed it to me through my window rather than bringing it to my door. Finally, a couple of hours after lunch, I was told I could come out of my bedroom. They did not let me go down the hall toward room 7.

The next day, September 15, I was sent back outside to work for the first time since the CNN interview. I was pretty sure someone new had arrived in the labor camp, but I never saw him. *Well, if someone is here, I may not be able to see him, but he can hear me from outside. His window has to be open just like mine*, I thought.

I started singing loudly in English, "God is so good." I paused and listened, hoping whoever was hearing might sing along with me to let me know they were there.

I didn't hear anything.

After a couple of days of trying to make contact, I asked one of the guards, "So who is in room 7?"

"No one," he snapped.

"Come on. I know someone is there. I heard someone cough a few times."

"Nobody coughed," he said.

"I even saw you bring two trays of food in during lunch. Someone else has to be here," I said.

"No. Nobody is there. You are the only prisoner in the camp."

I didn't argue the point.

The same day I had this conversation, the warden came to me and asked about my health. I went down my usual list of ailments.

He replied, "Maybe we should think about sending you to the hospital."

This was on a Tuesday. That Friday he asked me the same questions and ended the conversation by saying, "I think it is time for you to go spend some time in the hospital. You have lost a lot of weight."

In my two months back at the labor camp, I had dropped twenty-five pounds. I had lost ten just since the CNN interview. The warden's questions made me think something had to be up, but the rest of the day passed and nothing happened.

The next day, Saturday, September 20, I went outside and worked all day. I dug up rocks from the streambed and carried them back to the front of the building. The weather was scorching hot, and I was covered in sweat. Around three in the afternoon, the guards suddenly took me back to my room.

The warden was waiting there for me. "You're leaving to go back to the hospital. So pack now."

I still had not seen the newest prisoner, so I asked the warden about him, telling him that I had hoped I might have some company working out in the field.

"What other person?" the warden asked. "There is nobody else here but you."

Later I learned that Matthew Miller started working in the field the Monday after I left the camp.

When I left my room, several guards met me in the hallway to tell me good-bye. I found it hard to say good-bye to some of them. One told me, "You know, under different circumstances, I think we could have been good friends." I agreed.

Because no one had ever been in the camp three times, I felt it very unlikely I was going to come back for a fourth. Every parting had felt like the last good-bye, but this one really did. I felt very strongly that, barring an act of God, this was the last time I was ever going to see these guys. I prayed in my heart for them and hoped that my time with them might bear fruit.

On the drive back to the hospital I allowed my hopes to go up, thinking my nightmare might finally be coming to an end. When we arrived I was ushered back to the same room and given the same diagnosis. I had malnutrition—again. My bad back was still bad. My arm still hurt. I woke up every hour because of numbness and sharp pain in my hands. With the exception of my diabetes, everything that had been wrong with me on April 30, 2013, when I was first sent to the labor camp, was still wrong with me now.

The doctor prescribed rest, rest, and more rest. Her prescription struck me as funny because the camp doctor always prescribed work, work, and more work as the cure for everything wrong with me. I did get the feeling that they wanted me to be in peak health for some reason. I hoped the reason was my release.

Mr. Disappointment did his best to destroy my hopes of release. He came to see me in the hospital, and just as he had done for a year, he told me, "Nothing is being done to get you home. Your government has forgotten you. People have moved on. You are going to be here a long time. I will treat you to some special noodles on your sixtieth birthday."

As September ended and October wore on with no apparent changes in my situation, I found it hard not to believe him, even though I still received mail from my family telling me to stay strong.

As time dragged by I didn't think about giving up. Instead, I found myself tempted to become what the North Koreans had always accused me of being. More than once I told myself, *If I don't get out this year, maybe I will become a freedom fighter.*

I had asked God to make me a bridge to North Korea. Now I didn't care about being a bridge. I was angry about all I saw in this country. Every day I still had to sit in front of a television, watching more of their propaganda. A year earlier I had found their lies annoying. Now they made me very angry.

If I ever get out of here, maybe I will become the spokesman for human rights they fear I might become. I will let the world know the truth of how this entire country is enslaved by a system of lies.

In my earlier interactions with Mr. Park, Mr. Lee, Mr. Min, and even Mr. Disappointment, I had done my best to maintain a gentle and humble spirit. I wanted to show people Jesus to open their hearts to him. Now I was ready to become one of the prophets of old.

I'm just going to start preaching the gospel really loud and see what happens, I told myself.

October was a real spiritual struggle for me. I prayed less than I ever had since I was arrested. Nor was I reading the Bible as much. Over the course of the two years I was in North Korea, I read the Bible through seventeen times. Now I hardly touched it. I was depressed. I was angry. I was tired and ready to go home.

And then Mr. Disappointment came in and started in on his "No one cares about you, no one remembers you, you are never going home" speech. It was nearly more than I could bear. I wanted to tell him what my mother always had told me: "If you can't say anything nice, don't say anything at all."

The two-year anniversary of my arrest was just around the corner. I did not know how much more I could take. *Oh, Lord, help me*, I prayed. *I am at the end of my rope.*

I Will Bring You Home

"Because he loves me," says the LORD, "I will rescue him;
I will protect him, for he acknowledges my name."
—Psalm 91:14

ON SATURDAY, NOVEMBER 1, 2014, Mr. Disappointment came into my room for his weekly pep talk. His message had not changed: "No one is coming for you. No one remembers you. You are going to be here until we celebrate your sixtieth birthday together."

I did not respond. I just listened and hoped he would leave soon. His message hit me hard. Since the day I returned to the hospital, I had hoped a special envoy from the United States was on its way. Six weeks had passed without the slightest hint that one was going to come. After Mr. Disappointment left, I spent the rest of the day down and depressed.

I woke up Sunday, November 2, realizing I had to make a choice. I could either listen to Mr. Disappointment, or I could listen to the voice of God. I started to grab my Bible, but for some reason I picked up the stack of more than three hundred letters I had received from people all over the world. Mr. Disappointment had worn me down by telling me I was forgotten. Then I read a note from a family in Northern Ireland:

"You are not forgotten, Kenneth, so we stand with you and your family to get justice for you. Keep looking up, Kenneth."

Another letter from Tina, whom I have never met, said, "I pray for you to stay strong. Don't be defeated. You need to stay strong. Don't give up your fight."

Nick from Seattle told me, "Remember that no one can hurt your soul. I pray that you would feel the presence of God all the time. Thank you for your courage and your love for the North Korean people."

Tears flooded my eyes as I read. I wiped them away and kept reading. "I struggle to understand what the reason must be for you to endure such hardship," Jennifer wrote. "All I can offer you is that your story is giving many, many people hope and a renewed sense of faith here in the U.S." *God bless Jennifer M.*, I prayed.

Anna wrote to reassure me, "God is good. Yes, in the midst of this severe pain, God is still good. He is still just. He is still on his throne . . . I don't know if this e-mail will help you in any way. I don't know if it will even be read. But just in case it is read and it serves as a reminder of the greatness of God, I thought I'd send it."

Kelly wrote, "I encourage you today to stay committed to the 'mission' laid on your heart. That mission of compassion."

Yes, Lord, I am a missionary, and I was sent here for a reason, I prayed.

I spent most of my morning reading letters from supporters I had never met. After an hour or so, I laid them down and got down on my face before God.

Lord, I need your peace, I prayed. *I need your strength. You said that when we are weak, you are strong. I need you to fill me with your strength today, Lord, because I feel very weak.*

The more I prayed, and the more letters I read, the less I heard the voice of Mr. Disappointment and the more I heard the voice of God. I didn't know how much more I was going to have to endure, but I knew through God's strength I would make it. Too many people were praying for me; I would not fail.

The next morning, Monday, November 3, I awoke at six o'clock.

I had never awoken that early in the hospital, but I was wide-awake. Then I heard the voice of the Spirit of God say to me, *Open your Bible to Zephaniah 3:20.* I had no idea what Zephaniah 3:20 said. Hope washed over me as I read the first two lines:

> At that time I will gather you;
>> at that time *I will bring you home.*

In my spirit I sensed God say, *Now is the time. Now I will bring you home.*

Four days later, on Friday, November 7, around 9:30 p.m., Mr. Disappointment came to see me. He had never come at such a late hour before.

"You're going to have another interview tomorrow morning," he said. "You need to be up and ready to go by 7:30. But this time, instead of pleading with the United States for help, you need to thank the North Korean government for treating you so well and apologize one more time for what you have done. Maybe this will be the last thing you will have to do before you go home."

"Does this mean someone came from the US government?" I asked, hopeful.

"No. No one came. It's just an interview," he said.

"With whom? CNN again?" I asked.

"I don't know. But if you do well, maybe good things will happen. Prepare yourself tonight so that you can do a good job tomorrow," Mr. Disappointment said.

I could not sleep that night. *He never comes this late. And I have never done an interview at 7:30 in the morning. This must be urgent. Something must be up.* Then I remembered that a flight from Beijing lands in Pyongyang at six in the evening. Maybe someone had come on that flight, and that's why Mr. Disappointment came to see me so late. The flight out of Pyongyang back to Beijing leaves at ten in the morning. Maybe I had to do an early interview to make the flight.

These thoughts ran through my head all night. I think I dozed off for two or three hours at the most.

Mr. Disappointment walked in right on time the next morning. He took one look around and asked, "Why didn't you pack?"

"You didn't tell me to pack," I said.

"Don't worry about it. We will pack for you." He handed me some clothes. "Here is a clean prison uniform. You need to put this on."

"Okay," I said. I knew this meant that I was either going home or going back to the prison camp.

A van took me to the Potonggang Hotel, where Mr. Disappointment and a group of guards escorted me to a suite. My mother had stayed at this very hotel one year earlier when she came to see me. On the drive to the hotel, my sense of anticipation rose. The guards were decked out in their dress uniforms. I took that as a good sign.

Once we got into the suite, Mr. Disappointment told me, "Take a seat." It was around eight o'clock.

Forty-five minutes later, three American men walked in. One was Korean American. One of the other men, who was perhaps fifty, stepped over and told me he was a doctor.

"We are from the United States government," he said. "We are here to check on your health." He asked a few questions about my conditions. While the doctor examined me, no one talked. I remained silent except to answer his questions. The guard and Mr. Disappointment sat back and observed what was going on.

After twenty minutes the doctor said he was finished. "Good luck to you, sir," the doctor said, and the three men left.

I sat down and looked over at Mr. Disappointment. He seemed quite relaxed. It was now after nine o'clock. He never mentioned going out to do an interview. Apparently, all we were going to do was sit in this room. One guard looked at his watch.

"It's okay," I said, "I've waited two years. I can wait a little while longer."

"Don't get your hopes up too high, or you will be disappointed," he said with care.

By noon Mr. Disappointment dismissed himself and left me in the room with just one guard. I knew the guard from the labor camp. A little before one o'clock, room service delivered a meal. The guard and I ate together, which was a first for me. I said to him, "Hey, this is our first and last meal together."

"Don't say that," he replied. "You are making me sad. Don't say that."

Finally, at three o'clock, Mr. Disappointment returned.

"Let's go," he said.

I didn't even have time to tell the guard good-bye. We rushed out of the room and down the hall. I expected to go to another room in the hotel, perhaps a conference room. Instead, he led me out of the hotel and to a waiting van. This was not what I expected. I did not know if I was going back to the hospital, back to the labor camp, or somewhere else. The van's windows were covered, so I could not see where we were going.

When the van finally stopped, the doors opened, and I saw the Koryo Hotel in front of me. I knew this place well. I had stayed here three times in 2012, when I was still a free man and welcome guest of the DPRK. Mr. Disappointment led me upstairs to a conference room on the second floor. I did not know what was waiting for me inside. My first meeting with the Swedish ambassador had taken place in a hotel conference room. That's also where I had called my family. I half expected to see the Swedes when the doors opened.

Instead, waiting in the room for me was the prison warden in his full military uniform. He rarely ever wore the uniform at the prison, although he was officially an army officer. A few other officials were also in the room. All wore uniforms or other official clothes.

The warden came over and said, "I am pleased to inform you, 103, that the Marshal, Kim Jong Un himself, has decided to show you mercy and grant you a special pardon."

The weight of the world lifted off my shoulders. For two years I had waited to hear these words. Tears welled up, but I pushed them back.

"You are to sit down and write a letter of apology and a letter of thanksgiving to the Marshal," the warden continued.

"Yes, sir," I said with a smile. I sat down and wrote the letters in a hurry. Another official, whom I did not know, picked up the letters, looked them over, and seemed satisfied.

"Come with us," a guard said. Another guard came up on the other side of me, and the two took me to the room next door. It was now three thirty. When I walked in I saw Matthew Miller standing with two other guards. I did not yet know his name, but I knew he had to be the other prisoner from the camp. Like me, he wore a prison uniform, but his had 107 on the front.

A moment later a North Korean delegation entered the room and sat at a large conference table. The man I took to be the leader told the others not to stand when the American delegation entered the room.

A few minutes later eight Americans walked into the room. Five took seats at the table, while the other two men and the doctor who had come to see me earlier stood behind them. The primary US envoy was James Clapper, the director of national intelligence, a cabinet-level position.

The eight Americans all had very stern looks on their faces, as if they were upset. Only after I was back in the United States did I learn that the North Koreans had left the delegation hanging for a couple of days. Up until three o'clock the Americans didn't know whether I was going to be released to them. Looking at their stern expressions, I felt like a little child sitting in the principal's office, in trouble. The delegation was my parent who had to come to apologize on my behalf. I felt so sorry for the headaches I had caused, but, at the same moment, I had never been more thankful or proud to be a citizen of the United States of America.

Once the American delegation was in place, a one-star general of the DPRK army walked in and shouted at the top of his lungs, "Everybody stand!"

A four-star general then entered the room. Later I learned that he was Kim Won Hong, the director of their national security bureau, and the man responsible for the death of Kim Jong Un's uncle, Jang Song Thaek. The general unfurled a paper that looked like a piece of parchment and proceeded to read a special proclamation from Kim Jong Un himself.

"By order of the Marshal of the Democratic People's Republic of Korea, the American criminal Bae Junho is hereby pardoned. Signed by the Marshal himself on the sixth day of November, two thousand fourteen," he read in a stern voice.

A translator immediately repeated the proclamation in English. A similar proclamation was read for Matthew Miller.

As I listened to the proclamation it hit me: Today was November 8. The envoy probably had not arrived until the day before, November 7. Everything had already been decided even before the American delegation arrived.

After the proclamation was read, the ceremony came to an end. The guards escorted me to another room, where I was allowed to change out of the prison uniform and into my real clothes.

The warden came in to say good-bye. He grabbed my hand, shook it, and said with tears in his eyes, "I want to see you again sometime."

"Yes," I said, "I would like to come back and see you as well." I was touched that he became so emotional. The two of us had spent a great deal of time talking about a variety of topics. He was a very educated man. I guess our talks meant a lot to him.

Mr. Disappointment also came in to say good-bye. I couldn't help but ask, "Why did you keep telling me that no one remembered me and that I was never going to get to go home?"

"I did that for you," he said. "I did not want you to get your hopes up only to have them crushed."

I just smiled and shook my head. "Well, good-bye then," I said to him.

Once I had changed clothes, I was officially handed over to the American delegation. All of us were whisked out of the hotel. Matthew Miller, the doctor, and I were ushered into a waiting bus. The rest of the delegation climbed into waiting limos. I was so excited that I do not remember if we even talked on the ride to the airport. At least, I hoped we were headed toward the airport. I did not take anything for granted. I wasn't going to believe I was actually going home until the wheels of the plane lifted off the ground.

The bus arrived at the airport a little after four o'clock. We did not stop but kept right on driving across the tarmac and down one of the runways. I looked to see where we were going, but I couldn't quite tell. It was nice to be able to actually look out the window of a moving vehicle.

About ten minutes later the bus finally came to a stop. There, sitting on the runway, door open with a stairway waiting for me, was an airplane with the words *United States of America* emblazoned on the side. It was the most amazing thing I had ever seen in my life.

Now I could finally believe it. I was on my way home.

Once we had taken off, a woman asked how I was doing. "I am Alison Hooker. I work as a director of the Korea desk at the National Security Council in the White House," she said with a smile. She said that she was a Christian who had followed my story closely.

"I cannot tell you how thankful I am to be on this plane," I said. "It has been such a long wait. I nearly gave up hope. But on Monday, November 3, the two-year anniversary of my arrest, the Lord spoke to me through Zephaniah 3:20 and told me he was going to bring me home."

She looked at me, her mouth wide open in shock. "We left Washington, DC, on Monday," she said. "But we had some mechanical problems and had to make a stop in Hawaii. It took them two days to fix the plane."

I also asked her, "Have they asked for the medical bill? How much did it come out to?" I was worried about the bill. According to my calculation, it could be close to $300,000.

She said, "They never mentioned a bill. We did not have to pay anything."

I smiled. The last burden I carried out of North Korea was lifted.

I sat back in my seat and reflected on the past week. Monday had been one of the lowest days of my life. Yet the Lord already had his rescue on the way. I just needed to trust him.

That was the lesson I had learned across the entire two-year experience. Rather than panic or become afraid or angry, all I needed to do was trust the Lord. There were days when I had felt so alone, so forgotten. But God had not forgotten me. He was still in control of all things. He had a plan, and he worked it out beautifully in his time.

And we know that in all things God works for the good of those who love him, who have been called according to his purpose.

—Romans 8:28

EPILOGUE

ON NOVEMBER 8, 2014, I finally left North Korea after 735 days of detainment. I now hold the distinction of being the longest-held American detainee since the Korean War.

On the flight home the first meal I ate was a grilled cheese sandwich and some French onion soup. To me, they tasted like America.

After stops in Guam and Hawaii, we landed at Joint Base Lewis-McChord, near Seattle, Washington, nearly twenty-one hours after we took off from Pyongyang.

As I deplaned, I saw my mom walking toward me. I walked as fast as I could and gave her a big hug.

"Hi, Mom," I said.

My sister, Terri, came running up behind her, followed by her husband, Andy, and two of my nieces, Ella and Caitlin. I tried to wrap my arms around all of them. Tears flowed. For two years I had dreamed of this moment, and now I was finally back with my family and friends. After seeing them and embracing them, I finally realized that I was really free.

After a brief reunion, Terri told me a lot of reporters were waiting for me to make a statement in the press conference room. I told her that I would make a very brief statement. I wanted to thank everyone who was involved in getting me released as well as those who signed petitions and interceded for me daily.

At the press conference, I said that it had been "an amazing two years." But I did not explain why. What I wanted to say was that God had been amazingly faithful, and his grace was sufficient, and his compassion for the lost is everlasting.

As I look back a year later, I realize that in North Korea I learned God's faithfulness, experienced his grace, and witnessed his compassion in ways I never had imagined before. I learned to trust God and to hold on to his promises. When I was weak, he was strong. He kept his word, and his word was absolutely binding. As he promised, he never left me nor forsook me. Although I had moments when I was depressed and had lost hope, and I sometimes felt abandoned and forgotten by the world, God was there. Even when I doubted God's promises, he was faithful. When I needed it most, he reminded me he was there. He spoke through scriptures and supernatural encounters and even by giving me something as simple as a bowl of cold noodle soup. He truly is the same yesterday, today, and forever.

Before my arrest in North Korea, I had thought I understood these things, and I had thought I knew God intimately. But through enduring hardships with him, God took our relationship to a whole new level. I discovered that when you hold on to God's promises, they truly do give you hope—and hope gives life. As Psalm 119:50 says, "My comfort in my suffering is this: Your promise preserves my life." Yes, Jesus was my hope, and he is the hope I've built my life upon.

During my captivity I also learned I must give up my rights if I really trust God. My life must be about his will and plan, not mine. He is sovereign God, and his plan is always better than mine. I learned to stand at his feet during the time of trial and hardship. I learned that Jesus is worth living for. He is even worth going to prison for. I would not have learned that otherwise. I finally realized what it means to rejoice in suffering, especially suffering for the sake of his Name. I received the rare honor of suffering disgrace for his Name. I experienced the power of Acts 5:41, which says, "The apostles left the Sanhedrin, rejoicing because they had been counted worthy of suffering disgrace for the Name."

My two years in North Korea also taught me what it means to have compassion for those who live in darkness. People in North Korea have no access to information from the outside world, no freedom to travel, no freedom to speak their own minds, and no way to choose their own religions. More than one person told me that they have to trade their freedom in order to sustain their way of life. They prefer the safety in the dark, under the protection of a totalitarian regime, to the dangers freedom brings. That's why someone like me, who raises questions about the structure of their society, is a potential threat to the nation.

Since they are cut off from the rest of the world, the people in the DPRK are often forgotten by the world, yet they are remembered by God, just as he remembered me during my captivity. He has compassion for North Korea, just as he poured out his compassion on me. In my conversations with the interrogators, the prosecutors, the guards, and even Mr. Disappointment, I felt the heart of God. He loves them. He cares for them. He remembers them. He sees their tears, and he hears their cries. During my two years of detainment in North Korea, I felt the heart of God longing to restore his people once again.

I am eternally grateful to the hundreds of thousands of people who prayed for me every day. During my press conference, I said, "I am standing strong because of you." Because of the prayers of people around the world, I was able to endure my trials and continue to have hope to be released. Those prayers not only brought me home but also enabled me to stand strong. My victory was our victory. I not only came home but I came home stronger than ever. I felt as if I had been on a personal retreat with the Lord for two years.

But now these prayers need to continue. The Lord also reminded me that people of God should not forget the people trapped in darkness, such as those in North Korea. We must always remember the forgotten people through prayer and through acts of compassion. I organized tours to bring three hundred Christians to North Korea to pray, believing that someday the spiritual wall that surrounds the country will fall. I ask the hundreds of thousands of people who prayed for me to now pray for North Korea as well. Their prayers carried me through the darkest time of my life. Now we must pray for the release of all those living in darkness.

In North Korea, more than twenty-four million people live with no knowledge of the one true God. I can still hear the question of the guard in Rason ringing in my ears: "Where does this Jesus live, in China or in Korea?" He is not alone in the darkness. More than a billion people worldwide still have not heard the gospel. They do not have a Bible in their own language. We must remember them, pray for them, and build a bridge to them through which we can share God's love and compassion.

I pray that I can still become a bridge to connect North Korea to the rest of the world. I pray that someday the DPRK will welcome a missionary who can openly share God's heart for their nation. As I write this book, I dream that missionary might be me. I am thankful for the compassion and care that was shown to me by the staff at the hospital and at the labor camp. Someday I hope to return there and thank them in person. But I don't want to be the only bridge. I hope and pray that Christians around the world will remember and embrace the people of North Korea and, through prayer, become a bridge of blessings that only come from God. May God be their God, and may they be his people.

"This is the covenant I will make with the people of Israel
after that time," declares the LORD.
"I will put my law in their minds
and write it on their hearts.
I will be their God,
and they will be my people.
No longer will they teach their neighbor,
or say to one another, 'Know the LORD,'
because they will all know me,
from the least of them to the greatest,"
declares the LORD.
"For I will forgive their wickedness
and will remember their sins no more."

—JEREMIAH 31:33–34

ACKNOWLEDGMENTS ———————————

I CANNOT FIND the words to describe how much I am thankful to the thousands upon thousands of people who worked to secure my freedom, beginning with those who prayed continually for my release. I may not be able to list everyone's names, but I want you to know how deeply grateful I am for all of you. Through the power of your prayers I was able to stand strong, and your prayers brought me home. Thank you.

I am deeply thankful to President Obama and secretary of state John Kerry for securing my release. Thank you also to director of intelligence James Clapper, Alison Hooker, and everyone who came to North Korea and brought me home. They spent an entire week on a plane just trying to get to me. I will never forget the moment when they entered the conference room in Pyongyang. I was never so proud and happy to be an American.

I must also thank many others at the State Department who have worked tirelessly behind the scenes for my freedom, especially assistant secretary Wendy Sherman, ambassador Robert King, ambassador Glyn Davies, Linda McFadyen, Kate Rebholz, and Michael Clausen. Thank you for your hard work and also for caring for my family during my imprisonment. And I want to thank all those at the US consulates in Shenyang and Beijing who helped and cared for my family in China during my detainment.

To the Swedish embassy in Pyongyang: ambassador Karl-Olof Andersson, John Svensson, and Cecilia Anderberg, I thank you for your personal care and for your advocacy during the two years of my detainment. I am eternally grateful for you. May the Lord bless you.

I also want to recognize Washington congressman Rick Larsen, senator Patty Murray, and senator Maria Cantwell, as well as congressman Charles Rangel of New York and former governor of New Mexico and UN ambassador Bill Richardson for advocating for my freedom.

I want to thank Rev. Jesse Jackson and his colleague Grace Ji-Sun Kim for advocating for me, writing eleven letters to the North Korean government, and offering yourself as an envoy to bring me home. May the Lord continue to bless you and use you as an instrument for God's kingdom.

I owe eternal gratitude to Bobby Lee; John Thomas; Laura Choi and her husband, Isaac Choi; and Kelly Sadler for starting, maintaining, and promoting FreeKenNow.com and the Facebook page for me. Each day, they spent hours updating and sharing new information regarding my imprisonment. Thank you, Bobby, for running a marathon carrying a "Free Ken Now" sign on your back. Thank you for the two-year-long marathon you endured and finished on my behalf.

I want to acknowledge Derek Sciba for spending countless hours helping my sister manage media relations and press releases and for being such an amazing friend to my family. Thank you, Pastor Eugene Cho, for your indispensible advice and support during my imprisonment and beyond.

A heartfelt thank you to Euna Lee for starting the Letters for Kenneth campaign and for being there for me as a sister in Christ even though we had never met. Your compassion and caring letters sustained me throughout my imprisonment. To Lisa Ling, I thank you for your care and help. I also want to thank all those who have sent me letters through the Letters for Kenneth campaign. Altogether I received more than 450 letters from people around the world whom I had never met. I read your letters dozens of times, and each time I was reminded that I was not forgotten or alone. You stood together with me during my darkest time of my life. Because of your letters and prayers, I was able to stand firm and endure the hardships I faced. Thank you.

I also want to thank David Sugarman for caring for my family and advocating for my release through launching the #BringBaeBack campaign. Even though we had never met, you poured your heart and soul into efforts to bring me home, and I am moved beyond words. I also want to thank the 177,512 people who signed my son's Change.org petition. Every signature reassured me that I was not forgotten.

I must also thank all those who made this book a reality. To Mark Tabb, I appreciate you for helping to make my story come alive for readers. It has been wonderful to know you and your family during the writing process.

To my publisher and editors, Joel Kneedler and Meaghan Porter, I thank you for allowing me to tell the story to the world, and I truly appreciate your genuine heart for believing in the story of God. I thank Judy McDonough and everyone else at W Publishing/Thomas Nelson for putting this book together.

To my agent, Bryan Norman, I thank you for your dedication, your hard work, and for believing my story needed to be told to the world. I thank everyone at Alive Literary Agency.

Finally, I want to thank my sister, Terri, for her unfailing dedication to get me home. She literally spent thousands of hours writing letters, appearing on news channels, traveling to meet government officials, and working with experts on North Korea and community leaders. She became my voice when I could not speak. She never gave up my fight, and she never let anybody forget about my plight. If not for my sister, I might still be in the labor camp—or worse.

I also want to thank my parents for enduring such hardship and for their sustained and deepened faith in the Lord. It was a tremendously difficult time for them, yet they stood firm and never wavered in their hope to bring me home. I thank you.

To my wife, Lydia, I have caused you such heartache, but you always remained strong in your faith and waited for me while seeking God's strength. To my children— Jonathan, Sophia, and Natalie—I love you all, and thank you for not losing hope and praying for my release. I often looked at your pictures and reminded myself that I have a family to go back to. All of you were a reason for me to endure.

Most of all, thank you, Lord Jesus, for bringing me home and helping me to know you deeper during my imprisonment. Thank you for meeting me in my times of trouble and sustaining me when I could not go on any longer. Thank you for using me as your instrument even in the darkest time of my life. I love you.

NOTES

CHAPTER 15: THE WHOLE WORLD NOW KNOWS

1. Dana Ford, Jethro Mullen, and K. J. Kwon, "'He's Not a Spy,' Says Sister of U.S. Man Sentenced in North Korea," CNN, May 3, 2013, http://www.cnn.com/2013/05/02/world/asia/north-korea-american-sentenced.

2. Jonathan Bae, "Amnesty for my Father Kenneth Bae, a U.S. Citizen Imprisoned in a North Korean Special Labor Camp," Change.org, accessed December 4, 2015, https://www.change.org/p/amnesty-for-my-father-kenneth-bae-a-u-s-citizen-imprisoned-in-a-north-korean-special-labor-camp.

3. Dennis Rodman, tweet posted May 7, 2013, by @dennisrodman, https://twitter.com/dennisrodman/status/331826019747127297.

CHAPTER 17: I AM A MISSIONARY

1. Rick Warren, *The Purpose Driven Life: What on Earth Am I Here For?* (Grand Rapids: Zondervan, 2002), 286.

2. Ibid., 194.

3. Kyle Idleman, *Not a Fan: Becoming a Completely Committed Follower of Jesus* (Grand Rapids: Zondervan, 2001), 151–52.

CHAPTER 19: MORE DISAPPOINTMENT

1. Michael Martina, "Rodman Back from North Korea, Without Jailed American," Reuters, September 7, 2013, http://www.reuters.com/article/us-korea-north-rodman-idUSBRE98602B20130907#WziksV6hzh5Tqeae.97.

2. Dennis Rodman, interview by Chris Cuomo, *CNN New Day*, January 7, 2014, http://www.cnn.com/videos/world/2014/01/07/newday-cuomo-dennis-rodman-kenneth-bae-cutdown.cnn.

3. Stephen Rex Brown, "Dennis Rodman: 'Sorry, I Was Drunk,'" *New York Daily News*, January 9, 2014, http://www.nydailynews.com/news/world /dennis-rodman-apologizes-kenneth-bae-family-article-1.1570687.

4. Terri Chung, interview by Anderson Cooper, *AC360°*, January 7, 2014, http://www.cnn.com/videos/world/2014/01/08/ac-terri-chung-kenneth -bae-north-korea-rodman.cnn.

5. Shin Se-min, "U.S. President Obama Calls for Detained American Kenneth Bae to Be Released," Arirang News, February 6, 2014, https:// www.youtube.com/watch?v=vTSyrnIPXe8.

CHAPTER 21: IS THAT WHAT IS GOING TO HAPPEN TO ME?

1. "Where Jesus Is, 'Tis Heaven," lyrics by Charles J. Butler (1898), music by James Milton Black (1898), http://www.hymnary.org/media /fetch/127505.

ABOUT THE AUTHORS

KENNETH BAE was born in Seoul, Korea, on August 1, 1968. His family immigrated to the United States in 1985. Kenneth went to high school in California and attended the University of Oregon and Covenant Theological Seminary in St. Louis, Missouri. He held multiple jobs in sales and marketing until he moved to China in 2006. After years of managing his cultural-exchange business and missionary work, he transitioned into the travel and tourism industry in 2010, planning trips to North Korea. Kenneth had a passion to introduce Westerners to the untainted beauty of the landscape and people of North Korea and was excited to contribute to their economic development.

He is a licensed preacher in the Presbyterian Church in America (PCA), is an ordained Southern Baptist pastor, and has been working with Youth With A Mission (YWAM) since 2005. Kenneth is a husband and a father of three children aged nineteen to twenty-six.

MARK TABB has authored or coauthored more than thirty books, including the number one *New York Times* bestseller, *Mistaken Identity*.